Life Lines

PRESENTED TO:

_____

BY:

_____

DATE:

_____

OCCASION:

_____

Life Lines

Inspiration,
Insight,
and Wisdom
for
Daily Living

Dave Meyer

foreword by Joyce Meyer

WARNER
Faith

New York   Boston   Nashville

Life Lines

Warner Faith
Time Warner Book Group, 1271 Avenue of the Americas,
New York, NY 10020

Visit our website at www. twbookmark.com

The Warner Faith name and logo are registered trademarks
of Warner Books, Inc.

Printed in the United States of America.

First Printing: May 2004
10 9 8 7 6 5 4 3 2 1

ISBN: 0-446-52168-X
LCCN: 2004101218

CONTENTS

My husband, Dave Meyer, is one of the most stable people I have ever had the privilege of knowing. I have been married to Dave since 1966, and rarely have I witnessed him being anything other than peaceful and joyful. He has always been very positive and a man of few words. People who don't talk a lot often speak volumes when they do talk. Dave is one of those kinds of people. He sees things in a unique way—things that others often miss.

While I have always been more inclined to hurry through life and be satisfied with knowing the "bottom line" of things, Dave is extremely patient and given to details. I must admit that sometimes he says things that don't make sense to me at first. But when I really think about what he's saying, I discover a "gold mine" hidden in his statements.

Dave is a wise man. He uses tremendous wisdom in dealing with finances, and as a result, our ministry has always been able to operate completely debt free. His wisdom is evident not only in financial areas, but also in many others as well. In this book, you will find an extensive collection of what we call "Dave's Nuggets"— dynamic little statements that are full of power.

I encourage you to take your time and read this book slowly, pondering each page and meditating on what it says. Proverbs teaches us that wisdom is one of the most important things we are to seek. Without it life is a disaster. But with it we prosper and succeed in everything we do. Life is lengthened and we find favor with God and man. Dave has thoroughly enjoyed his life, which is rare among people today. I believe what he says is worth listening to, and I believe your joy and peace will increase as you apply these timeless words of wisdom to your life.

Joyce Meyer
Joyce Meyer Ministries

INTRODUCTION

What is a lifeline? *Webster's Collegiate Dictionary* (Eleventh Edition) states that it is "something regarded as indispensable for the maintaining or protection of life" and "a line used for saving or preserving life." In short, a lifeline is something we can't do without.

God's Word is our lifeline. It is our handbook for success on this earth—containing wisdom, counsel, direction, and strength for every situation we face. It is something to hold onto when times get tough. It's what pulls you up when the circumstances of life threaten to overwhelm you. It's the Source that shows you the way when there seems to be no way. The Psalmist put it well when he said, *Your word is a lamp to my feet and a light to my path* (Psalm 119:105).

Are you looking for answers to everyday life? Do you need encouragement for the road ahead? As I have sought God over the years, He has taught me many powerful lessons—lessons on character, grace, love, responsibility, faith, forgiveness, obedience, humility, prosperity, and every other facet of life—lessons that I am grateful to be able to share with you in this book.

I have organized this devotional into five different sections: Faith; Grace and Forgiveness; Character; Life in Christ; and Secrets of Daily Living. These are all areas that I believe are critical to growing in Christ and becoming all that God has intended for us to be.

God says in Jeremiah 33:3, *Call to Me and I will answer you and show you great and mighty things....* In Proverbs 8:17, He promises, *And those who seek me diligently will find me* (NKJV).

It is vitally important for each one of us to make an investment into God's Word. I've found that many people are looking for happiness and fulfillment, but they're willing to gamble with their lives and try many things that only lead them to ruin and devastation. However, when we invest our lives and our time into seeking God's ways and learning Kingdom principles, His Word promises that we will prosper and have good success (see Joshua 1:8). By doing things God's way, we can be happier than we ever imagined and reap dividends of joy, peace, satisfaction, mercy, contentment, and a life that gives glory to Jesus Christ.

I encourage you to incorporate these devotions into your daily time with God. Meditate on them. Pray about them. Allow God to use them to show you the "great and mighty things" He has for your life. As you do, I pray that you will enter into a greater relationship with Jesus Christ than you've ever known before. God bless you!

Dave Meyer

Life Line #1: FAITH

You don't know
what tomorrow holds,

BUT YOU DO KNOW
that God holds tomorrow.

God permits in His wisdom
WHAT HE COULD HAVE
altered or prevented in His power.

Though he slay me, yet will I trust in him.

JOB 13:15 KJV

WHO CAN IMAGINE the depths of grief or the suffering of the man whom God called "My servant Job"? His ten children perished. From head to toe his body was covered with boils and blisters. His staggering wealth vanished. His wife's only recorded words were a bitter directive to "renounce God and die!" Even his longtime friends, who should have brought comfort, and who should have known better, instead accused him of being a hypocrite in need of repentance. All because of Satan's hatred for Job, and because God was willing to allow Job's faith to be tested. "And the Lord said to Satan, Behold, he is in your hand; only spare his life" (Job 2:6).

As a believer, you know your faith will be tried, and Job's life demonstrates it can be tested to the extreme. You may taste of life's bitterness—you may taste more than you could have imagined—but hear God's word to your soul: "And we know that all things work together for good to them that love God, to them who are the called according to his purpose" (Romans 8:28 KJV). Come what may, know that through the Spirit's help God's purpose shall be accomplished. Rest in His unchanging wisdom!

The manifestation of great faith
   IS TO TRUST GOD
without having any indication
   of what you're *believing* God for.

If our God Whom we serve is able to deliver us
   from the burning fiery furnace,
He will deliver us out of your hand, O king.
   But if not, let it be known to you, O king,
      that we will not serve your gods
or worship the golden image which you have set up!

DANIEL 3:17, 18

KING NEBUCHADNEZZAR had never been addressed like this before. Three young Jewish men refused to fall before the image he had made, evidencing that their faith was greater than their sense of self-protection. It would have been so easy to avoid the king's fury. They could have said it meant nothing, that they were bowing the knee, not the heart. But because these men were holy, they were honest to the core.

These young men were not certain of the effect of their faith. But their faith had brought them face-to-face with God so the king's fiery furnace did not frighten them. To see the Almighty erases the fear of man. Our God is able to do exceeding abundantly above all that you ask or think. If you want to be the salt of the earth, be true to your faith no matter the cost.

God *wants you* to know that
   if you will do what you can do,
HE WILL DO
      what *you can't do*.

The Lord God is my Strength,
      my personal bravery, and my invincible army;
   He makes my feet like hinds' feet
and will make me to walk [not to stand still in terror,
      but to walk] and make [spiritual] progress
         upon my high places
   [of trouble, suffering, or responsibility]!

HABAKKUK 3:19

WHEN JESUS TOOK the boy's five barley loaves and two small fish and fed the five thousand (John 6), He demonstrated the transformation He works in your life when you are in touch with Him. Apart from Christ the bread was merely bread, but in His hands bread was linked to the divine. No matter how insignificant or weak or lacking in talent you feel, bring all that you are—body, soul, and spirit—and be joined to Christ. Never focus on your deficiencies. Only make sure you have given yourself fully to Christ. Allow Him to fill your mind with His Word and your heart with the love of Christ. Your abilities, great or small, when joined to Christ by faith, are sufficient for whatever He calls you to do.

In true faith,
the PROOF IS NOT
in the profession
but in the *procession.*

For in the Gospel a righteousness which God ascribes
is revealed, both springing from faith
and leading to faith [disclosed through the way of faith
that arouses to more faith]. As it is written,
The man who through faith is just and upright shall live
and shall live by faith.

ROMANS 1·17

UNTIL YOU SEE God face-to-face, you must live by simple faith in Him. Your righteousness both springs from faith and leads to more faith in the ever-living God. Your only source of continued spiritual life is the faith that draws all its sustenance from God. All self-efforts to save yourself and to overcome sin will utterly fail. Only the life and power of the Holy Spirit within you can save you from sin, and faith is the one condition of His working in you.

Abraham so believed God's promise that He offered up Isaac, trusting that God would raise Isaac from the dead. By faith Moses led the millions of Jews out of Egypt. By faith Joshua took them into the Promised Land despite fortified cities and giants. By faith the early church stood strong under persecution and could not be stopped. By faith you must move beyond profession into the procession.

True faith is timeless.
It can only be INTERRUPTED
by two things—*doubt*
or manifestation.

Jesus said, Take away the stone.
Martha, the sister of the dead man, exclaimed,
But Lord, by this time he [is decaying and] throws off an
offensive odor, for he has been dead four days!
Jesus said to her, Did I not tell you and promise you
that if you would believe and rely on Me,
you would see the glory of God?

JOHN 11:39, 40

THE STORY OF the raising of Lazarus from the dead is a beauty. Martha truly believed Lazarus would not have died if Jesus had been there sooner. She believed in Jesus as the Christ, her Messiah (John 11:21–27). But Jesus was about to take her faith to a new level—a level that defied any hint of natural possibilities. Faith must move beyond the theoretical to where it touches your deepest need at a level that requires the supernatural.

If Jesus could have spared Lazarus before his death, why not believe He would raise him from the dead after four days? Why not move beyond "could" do it to "will" do it? Take His promise and rest in it. You will see the glory of God!

The Bible does not tell you
      TO MAKE the Word work.
It tells you to *let the Word work.*

Moses told the people, Fear not; stand still
      (firm, confident, undismayed) and see the salvation
of the Lord which He will work for you today.
      For the Egyptians you have seen today
you shall never see again. The Lord will fight for you,
      and you shall hold your peace and remain at rest.

EXODUS 14:13, 14

THANK GOD FOR a leader like Moses. He saw the same impending crisis the people did and faced it with confidence in God's salvation. His courage rested upon his past experience of seeing God's deliverance based upon His word. This was a moment when faith alone would save them—all they had to do was stand still and let God do the fighting.

Perhaps you feel like the Israelites felt—walled in by an overwhelming problem that is absolutely real and threatening to destroy your life. You try to pray but fear grips your heart. You find yourself utterly helpless. It is a dangerous moment when human nature wants to break faith and complain against the Lord and blame someone else for the situation (Exodus 14:11, 12). By faith let God step in between you and the problem, and believe He will work it out.

Faith is now,
but the manifestation
IS IN DUE TIME.
So don't become *impatient.*

For you have need of steadfast patience and endurance,
so that you may perform and fully accomplish
the will of God, and thus receive and carry away
[and enjoy to the full] what is promised.

HEBREWS 10:36

THE HEBREW BELIEVERS were suffering deeply for their faith and the writer to the Hebrews was concerned that they not "fling away [their] fearless confidence, for it carries a great and glorious compensation of reward" (Hebrews 10:35). Faith must look beyond the present moment and tomorrow and your lifetime. Faith looks to eternity. You are a Christian for eternity, not for time. Weigh the eternal rewards coming your way against whatever losses you may suffer in this lifetime because of your faith in Christ. There is no comparison.

By His grace continue to patiently believe His Word and hold fast to the truth. The things you have believed, continue to believe. If the storms gather against you and the darkness descends, remember that the morning will dawn. Let your hope hear the distant hallelujahs that proclaim the coming reign of Christ. Rest in the assurance that the kingdom of God will win the day, even if you must step into eternity to enjoy it.

When *you* start sinking,
PAY ATTENTION
to what *you're thinking*.

Do not fret or have any anxiety about anything,
but in every circumstance and in everything,
by prayer and petition (definite requests),
with thanksgiving, continue to make
your wants known to God.

PHILIPPIANS 4:6

IF THERE'S ONE sure way to lose your peace and joy, it is to allow worries and anxieties to multiply in your life. There are a million and one things that cause anxiety, and if they reach your heart they weaken your faith, destroy your peace, and escalate into big problems. Apart from prayer, apart from being able to place everything in your life in the care of God, Paul's instruction is impossible.

The next time you feel you're sinking remind yourself that your Father in heaven is very experienced. For forty years He had no problem providing for every need of three million Israelites in the wilderness. Keep Him always in front of you. Turn your cares instantly into prayers and leave them with Him. Anchor your faith in God and discover the truth of what the English poet and hymn writer Frances Havergal wrote: "Those who trust Him wholly find Him wholly true."

If it's really faith,
YOU WILL NOT STRUGGLE;
you will enter God's rest
and let Him *deal with the trouble.*

For we who have believed (adhered to and trusted in
and relied on God) do enter that rest,
in accordance with His declaration
that those [who did not believe]
should not enter when He said, As I swore in My wrath,
They shall not enter My rest; and this He said although
[His] works had been completed and prepared
[and waiting for all who would believe] from
the foundation of the world.

HEBREWS 4:3

DESPITE THE GOOD news of Canaan's rest before them, the Israelites listened to the reports of giants in the land and saw themselves as grasshoppers. Had they had the faith of Caleb and Joshua they would have seen themselves as giants and the giants as grasshoppers. The good news of rest has come to you in Jesus Christ today—rest from the penalty of sin, rest from cares and anxieties. To rely upon Christ alone is no small matter. It involves your whole heart and soul. Christ is all you need and all you will ever need for your salvation. Beware of mixing any self-merit with your faith. Enter the rest of God and let God do the rest.

Waiting on the Lord
    is the ACTION OF FAITH.
Impatience is the fruit
        of the root *of pride.*

For God alone my soul waits in silence;
from Him comes my salvation.
He only is my Rock and my Salvation,
        my Defense and my Fortress,
I shall not be greatly moved.

PSALM 62:1, 2

THERE IS NOTHING passive about true faith. Faith is not merely nodding your head in agreement; it is the reverent commitment of your heart to embrace God. It actively stands through times of suffering and difficulties and refuses to be moved from God alone. At times your trust in Him will be strained by situations where God does not answer your prayers as expected and where disappointments and heartache tear at your beliefs. You need to be taught the lesson of patience, to not try to rise up as though you had the power to solve your situations without God, and to wait in silence before Him. The greatest pleasure you can give God is to trust your life and your concerns to Him with complete confidence. Stand still and wait upon Him and you shall see His salvation and your faith will be increased.

God will do whatever is required
to draw the impurities out of you
and get you to FACE THEM
so that He can deal with them
and *you can go free.*

But He knows the way that I take [He has concern for it,
appreciates, and pays attention to it].
When He has tried me, I shall come forth
as refined gold [pure and luminous].

JOB 23:10

READ THE STORY of Job and you'll see he was suffering at a level few people ever know. The loss of his family and his wealth and position was intensified by the severity of feeling that God had abandoned him for no cause. Yet Job reaches out in faith and declares that no matter how severely he is tested and refined by the fire, the day will come when God has gotten the last bit of dross out of him and he will be gold worthy of the King. That is marvelous faith, indeed! It is a profound thing to allow God to use whatever means necessary to draw the impurities out of you for ultimate blessing in your life as well as the lives of others. Find strength in the knowledge that God knows your way and will bring you forth as refined gold!

You must learn to be excited
WHEN YOU'RE BELIEVING,
not just when *you're receiving.*

They then said, What are we to do, that we may [habitually] be working the works of God? [What are we to do to carry out what God requires?] Jesus replied, This is the work (service) that God asks of you: that you believe in the One Whom He has sent [that you cleave to, trust, rely on, and have faith in His Messenger].

JOHN 6:28, 29

IT IS SECOND nature for us to think we must be busy doing the works of God, piling up points with every deed we accomplish. We only want to know how high the pile must get before we've done enough to please God. Jesus says that all the piles of works in the world count for nothing. One thing matters—that you believe in Him. You must first and foremost be a lover of Jesus. That changes everything. How exciting to know Him! When your faith is rooted in love, receiving and giving are natural, and chasing approval is out the window. To receive, believe rather than achieve.

Being in the will of God
    IS AN ATTITUDE, not a place.

Then said David to the Philistine, You come to me
with a sword, a spear, and a javelin, but I come to you
in the name of the Lord of hosts, the God
of the ranks of Israel, Whom you have defied.

1 SAMUEL 17:45

SOMEONE SHOULD HAVE warned Goliath that he didn't stand a chance against the young man named David. Nine-foot-nine-inch armor-clad giants who defy the living God should beware of slingshot-carrying young men who are walking in the center of God's will. While an entire army of Israelites ran from the presence of Goliath, waiting for someone else to intervene and get rid of the giant, David's attitude of faith was the touchstone of power that determined the outcome before the first rock was hurled.

In prayer, too many Christians wait for the outcome to determine their attitude when their attitude determines their outcome. You are more than a conqueror through Christ the Savior. Bring to bear the name of the Lord on whatever situation you confront and the power to overcome the world is at your disposal.

Fear of tomorrow, today,
     will produce TOMORROW
what you *fear today.*

The fear of man brings a snare,
        but whoever leans on, trusts in,
     and puts his confidence in the Lord
        is safe and set on high.

PROVERBS 29:25

WHENEVER YOU STEP up to do the will of God as the Jews who were rebuilding the temple after returning from the Babylonian Captivity were doing, you can expect opposition. "Then [the Samaritans] the people of the land [continually] weakened the hands of the people of Judah and troubled and terrified them in building" (Ezra 4:4). Why is it so easy for an evil person or a bad report to hinder the work of good men?

Fear comes in when you believe you can do nothing and neither can God. It is only as you see God that you can proceed with His work. If you take your eyes off Him, the fear of man will always take over and become a trap. Courage is rooted in having the eye of faith to see through the danger or the accusation or the criticism and know God's approval is all you need. Draw from the undefeatable confidence rooted in a conscience that knows the will of God and is determined to stay with it.

The difference between discouragement and encouragement IS DETERMINED BY WHOM you depend on—*God or man.*

There was a certain man there who had suffered with a deep-seated and lingering disorder for thirty-eight years. When Jesus noticed him lying there [helpless], knowing that he had already been a long time in that condition, He said to him, Do you want to become well? [Are you really in earnest about getting well?]

JOHN 5:5, 6

FOR THIRTY-EIGHT years this invalid had tried repeatedly to get into the healing waters, but with no one to help him it was hopeless. Of all those who had been healed at the pool not one remained to help him. Discouragement had taken over his life. His response to Jesus was not an immediate, "Yes, Lord," but a rambling of why he had not been healed.

If your faith is in others, discouragement from their failures to love and care for you will be inevitable. If your faith is in Jesus Christ, healing and wholeness are in Him for you. Jesus is an inexhaustible fountain of healing for whatever you need. Others may have left you behind, but Jesus seeks you out. Receive from Him the power to rise up and walk through the power of the Holy Spirit.

Believers are not to follow
AFTER SIGNS.
Signs are to *follow believers!*

Then Jesus said to him,
Unless you see signs and miracles happen,
you [people] never will believe (trust, have faith) at all.

JOHN 4:48

WE LIVE IN a generation where some believers will race from one meeting to another if "signs and wonders" are advertised. Wherever something "supernatural" is purported to be happening these folks will flock, even if it involves long miles and significant costs. One wonders if Jesus' exasperated words to the royal official, which must have felt like a bucket of cold water, are not applicable to what goes on today.

Why is it that so few see the beauty and grace of Christ's character, but so many are willing to race to Him for a miracle? Jesus tells the official to turn around and go home, that his son would live. Jesus wanted him to go beyond "seeing" a sign to trusting completely, and that is precisely what He wants you to do. Jesus said if you lovingly go about declaring His Gospel, signs will follow you rather than you chasing after them (Mark 16). Take His word alone as sufficient basis for your faith and go forth in strength.

You don't have victory if
you don't have problems.
YOU HAVE VICTORY
if your problems *don't have you.*

For whatever is born of God
is victorious over the world; and this is the victory
that conquers the world, even our faith.

1 JOHN 5:4

SATAN HAS ENTRENCHED himself as the ruler of this world, making earth a spiritual battlefield for the believer. There is an ongoing battle between truth and righteousness, and believers are often caught in the middle of the battle. On top of that, the world holds an attraction that can resurrect any person's desires and lusts, causing inner battles that afflict the soul.

The problems you face are constant and lifelong, and the only way to victory is a faith that lifts you above the problems. Faith empowers you to say no to the world's standards and lies and opinions. It frees you to live according to God's truth, even if doing so brings troubles and trials that could be avoided by compromise. Because you have been born of the Spirit of God, the power of the love of the world and its things has been broken. Take up the shield of faith that is mighty to bring supernatural change that will help you to stand to the end.

Are you trying out God, or
are you SOLD OUT TO GOD?
The difference is faith
instead of *hope so.*

*No unbelief or distrust made him waver (doubtingly
question) concerning the promise of God, but he
grew strong and was empowered by faith as he gave
praise and glory to God, fully satisfied and assured that
God was able and mighty to keep His word
and to do what He had promised.*

ROMANS 4:20, 21

IF YOU HAVE not surrendered your heart completely to God your faith will not stand up to what life brings your way. You can't try God out to see whether you like Him in your life or not. Faith, to be real, must totally rely or lean on God. Abraham had God's promise that he would bear a son but his physical disabilities made it seem impossible. Yet, "He did not weaken in faith when he considered the [utter] impotence of his own body, which was as good as dead because he was about a hundred years old, or [when he considered] the barrenness of Sarah's [deadened] womb" (Romans 4:19). He looked through the difficulty and believed that the word from God was greater. Join Abraham and know that because you believe your faith is reckoned to you as righteousness, a right standing with God!

If you believe you won't succeed
and don't, DON'T BLAME
someone else because
you won't believe *and don't.*

And Abel brought of the firstborn of his flock
and of the fat portions. And the Lord had respect
and regard for Abel and for his offering,
but for Cain and his offering He had no respect or regard.
So Cain was exceedingly angry and indignant....
And the Lord said to Cain, Why are you angry?...If you
do well, will you not be accepted?
And if you do not do well, sin crouches at your door;
its desire is for you, but you must master it.

GENESIS 4:4-7

THE DIFFERENCE BETWEEN Abel and Cain was in their hearts. Too much is made of the type of sacrifices they brought and too little of the fact God loves a cheerful giver. Abel brought his sacrifice as a reflection of a heart that knew its sin and was reaching out to God in faith for salvation (Hebrews 11:4). Cain refused to recognize his sin and brought his sacrifice without faith and was rejected by God. But rather than deal with the sin of his heart, Cain turned his unbelief and anger on his brother and killed him. Remember this: God never receives an offering from an unwilling, unbelieving heart.

When you live in the joy
and peace of abandonment,
you HAVE THE CONFIDENCE
that *all things* will work out
for your good *God's way.*

We are assured and know that [God being a partner
in their labor] all things work together and are
[fitting into a plan] for good to and for those who love God
and are called according to [His] design and purpose.

ROMANS 8:28

WHAT AN AMAZING statement for the apostle Paul to make! All things are working together for good in your life, like the gears of an engine moving in perfect harmony. If you love God, if you live in the joy and peace of abandonment to Him alone, you can know with utter certainty that God's love will make all things work together for His plan for your life. He is able to do this by "exerting that power which enables Him even to subject everything to Himself" (Philippians 3:21). Christ is constantly working to subdue anything that will obstruct His grand design and purpose. Bring this assurance to bear on whatever you sense the enemy is using to frustrate the work of God in your life. Rest in the faith that He is able to transform these problems to work for your good.

Are you letting
GOD BE GOD
or trying to help God *be God?*

And Hezekiah prayed: O Lord, the God of Israel,
Who [in symbol] is enthroned above the cherubim
[of the ark in the temple], You are the God, You alone,
of all the kingdoms of the earth. You have made
the heavens and the earth. Lord, bow down Your ear
and hear; Lord, open Your eyes and see; hear the words
of Sennacherib which he has sent to mock, reproach,
insult, and defy the living God.

2 KINGS 19:15, 16

KING SENNACHERIB of Assyria was about to destroy Jerusalem when King Hezekiah of Judah went into the house of the Lord, knelt before God and spread the blasphemous letter from Sennacherib before Him. Fortunately King Hezekiah had already learned to lean upon God with his faith. God's honor had been violated and Hezekiah could only plead that He intervene, which is precisely what happened. "That night the Angel of the Lord went forth and slew 185,000 in the camp of the Assyrians" (2 Kings 19:35). Hezekiah's prayer released God to be God.

Learn to lean, and God will show up on the scene.

If you want to
SENSE GOD'S DIRECTION
for your life,
you must give Him *your destiny.*

As for God, His way is perfect!
The word of the Lord is tested and tried;
He is a shield to all those who take refuge
and put their trust in Him.

PSALM 18:30

WHEN THE PROPHET Micaiah stood alone before King Ahab and King Jehoshaphat with the strong directive to agree with the lie that the 400 false prophets had already ratified, he immediately turned over his destiny to God. Micaiah's unflinching response was: "As the Lord lives, I will speak what the Lord says to me" (1 Kings 22:14). It was a moment of uncompromising commitment to God's way and the word of the Lord.

What are you willing to risk for your faith? Will you walk in the fear of false prophets and kings or will you follow His perfect way though the cost is great? Micaiah could have easily evaded a prison sentence (vs. 27), but he refused to accommodate the evil of the king's court. Thus, Micaiah was easily the most powerful man in the kingdom. To discover your destiny God will lead you to take your stand for the Word of the Lord. Learn what your faith is worth by refusing to compromise.

Life Line #2:
GRACE
and
FORGIVENESS

When you do something wrong,
do you try
to change yourself?

THAT IS GOD'S JOB.

The amount of energy
you spend trying
—*spend leaning*.

Prayer is the exercise
OF DRAWING ON
the grace *of God.*

All whom My Father gives (entrusts) to Me
will come to Me; and the one who comes to Me
I will most certainly not cast out [I will never,
no never, reject one of them who comes to Me].

JOHN 6:37

TO "COME" MEANS you have to leave something behind and go to something else. In this case you leave behind whatever you may have been trusting in and you come to Christ as your only source of hope. You come recognizing that it was the Father who loved you, who sent His Son to die for you—whether you are rich or poor, whether your sins are great or small, whether you are somebody or nobody.

In prayer you come to receive His grace. Grace that cleanses you from sin through His blood. Grace that brings eternal life through His Spirit. Grace that brings healing through His wounds. Grace that brings joy and peace through His presence. Grace that brings light to your darkness. To receive the grace of God, stop trying to get it.

CONVICTION IS MEANT
to convince you—*not condemn you.*

And when He comes, He will convict and convince
the world and bring demonstration to it about sin
and about righteousness (uprightness of heart and
right standing with God) and about judgment.

JOHN 16:8

THE HOLY SPIRIT convicts you of guilt by bringing the Law of God to bear on the sin in your heart. He turns His light on your soul and exposes the impurity within. His way is to convince you that what you have done or are doing is wrong, despite your repeated attempts to cover it over as though it is all right or not very wrong. If you are honest with yourself, you realize you try to justify your sins more than you care to admit.

Because He loves you, the Holy Spirit strives with you and thunders in your conscience, "Guilty! Guilty!" Anytime God convicts you His grace is available to restore you. If you yield to these strivings and confess your past sins He will pour in His grace of forgiveness and cleansing. He is continually working if you allow Him. Never quench the conviction of the Spirit!

Jesus will be Savior
without your behavior.
If you've allowed Him to be Savior,
He'll change your behavior.

But constantly and earnestly I bore testimony
both to Jews and Greeks, urging them to turn
in repentance [that is due] to God and to have faith
in our Lord Jesus Christ [that is due Him].

ACTS 20:21

THIS TEACHING OF Paul never changes. Where is there a human heart that can honestly say it does not need to repent? Who can read the Word of God and not be made aware of his or her sins and failures? How can anyone stand when the Holy Spirit turns His light upon their soul and exposes the darkness? How foolish it is to try to silence one's conscience and convictions.

How much better it is to confess your sin and put your faith in Jesus. Yet faith is the gift of God (Ephesians 2:8), not something you work up on your own. Faith is the opening of your spiritual eyes to see Him Who is invisible (Hebrews 11:27). Faith is the opening of your spiritual ears to hear the voice of God as He tells you of His grace. By faith refuse to live by your feelings but rather take hold of eternal truth and make it your own.

If the Word of God has been
HIDDEN IN YOUR HEART,
it will draw on the grace of God
in times *of trouble.*

My son, attend to my words; consent and submit
to my sayings. Let them not depart from your sight;
keep them in the center of your heart.
For they are life to those who find them,
healing and health to all their flesh.

PROVERBS 4:20–22

GOD'S WORD IS far more than a historic document. It was written by inspiration of the Holy Spirit long ago, but it has lost none of that inspiration for today. The Holy Spirit is in the Word, and the Word is, therefore, living truth. It is meant to be hidden in your heart and pondered in your mind that you might be rooted and grounded in its teaching and saturated in its spirit. It is the Father's book of grace for your soul.

The Pharisees were masters of the details of the Old Testament but they failed to take the words of God into their hearts. There was no link between the written Word and their hearts. It is possible to memorize the whole Bible and yet know nothing about God's revelation. If you want to find God's word in the Bible let it speak to your heart and allow it to become a revelation that is life to your soul.

Pride brings trouble
WHICH GOD USES
to pop *your bubble.*

When swelling and pride come,
then emptiness and shame come also,
but with the humble (those who are lowly,
who have been pruned or chiseled by trial,
and renounce self) are skillful and godly
Wisdom and soundness.

PROVERBS 11:2

THE PROVERBS ARE wise sayings based upon actual experience. Pride, Solomon assures us from having observed it and participated in it a thousand times, can only swell the head to a certain size and then comes the exposure of its emptiness and accompanying shame. It may strut itself around as though it deserves to be blessed but an inflated ego will be short-lived.

What is it that you think you have to be proud about? Your spiritual maturity, your intellect, your success? Get a grip on reality. What is it that you have that you did not receive? Unless you want God to burst your bubble, which He can do with surprising ease, remember that in and of yourself you are nothing, and that you are completely dependent upon God for everything. Nothing will ever change that. Humble your heart and renounce whatever is of self in your life and you shall be wise indeed.

You have no right
to steal God's glory—HIS GLORY
is a result of *His grace.*

I am the Lord; that is My name!
And My glory I will not give to another,
nor My praise to graven images.

ISAIAH 42:8

AFTER BEHOLDING ONE miracle after another in the deliverance of Israel from Egypt, Moses declared, "Who is like You, O Lord…glorious in holiness, awesome in splendor, doing wonders?" (Exodus 15:11). He is truly the Incomparable One Who not only triumphs over the enemy but Who in Christ Jesus came to dwell among mankind in His glory, "full of grace (favor, loving-kindness) and truth" (John 1:14), and redeemed sinners by His grace.

You were created to live for the praise and glory of God but how often do you try to steal His glory by claiming your works as your own? How foolish is that? Yet despite your sins God comes to you and humbles you so His name is not tainted. He cannot allow you to take credit for what is His alone. But God gives grace and glory to you freely. You have the glory of being His and serving Him and His glory in your soul. Humble yourself before Him, and may all your works be an expression of His gracious enabling.

Excuses are dangerous because
THEY CAN BLOCK
true *repentance.*

*He who heeds instruction and correction is
[not only himself] in the way of life [but also] is a way
of life for others. And he who neglects or refuses
reproof [not only himself] goes astray [but also]
causes to err and is a path toward ruin for others.*

PROVERBS 10:17

JESUS SAID THAT He "came that they may have and enjoy life, and have it in abundance (to the full, till it overflows)" (John 10:10). Solomon said you can know you are "in the way of life" if you are always prepared to accept instruction and correction. If you heed correction you acknowledge your mistakes and repent of your errors and resolve to stop doing them. If you are wise you heed correction and through instruction become wiser and full of the blessed life Jesus promised.

If you are stubborn when you are corrected and offer excuses for your sins rather than confessing and forsaking them, you harden your neck and continue down a pathway of ruin for yourself and for others. To stand still on the pathway of sin is impossible. The only direction it leads is into greater and greater darkness and decay. Never allow excuses to block the door to true repentance and pave the path to destruction.

God's grace is His power at work
   IN AND AROUND YOU
to keep you until you change,
      to *bring you* to the threshold
of change and to *change you.*

Do not be carried about by different and varied
      and alien teachings; for it is good for the heart
to be established and ennobled and strengthened
by means of grace (God's favor and spiritual blessing).

HEBREWS 13:9

EVERYTHING THAT COMES to you through your Lord Jesus, any blessing related to your salvation, is a gift of God's grace. You are never asked to pay for any portion of your forgiveness, justification, sanctification, or eternal life. God freely gives His grace. There are no "if" conditions written in front of it. And His grace extends to His power that is at work in your life today—power that is changing you, conforming you to the image of Jesus.

Remember that in freely giving you His grace God gives you Himself. He adopts you as His child and becomes your Father. He pardons your sin and gives you His righteousness. He gives you His love, His wisdom, and His power. He answers your prayers and comforts you in your sorrows. He gives you the Holy Spirit who dwells in you and empowers you to change. Receive them freely and without measure for these are all given without price.

Deal with situations.
Anything that you HIDE FROM
will eventually *find you.*

*And though they hide themselves on the top
of [Mount] Carmel, from there I will search out
and take them; and though they [try to] hide from
My sight at the bottom of the sea, there I will command
the serpent and it shall bite them.*

AMOS 9:3

EVER SINCE ADAM and Eve hid from God in the Garden of Eden, this expression has been true: "You can run but you can't hide." Does this sound familiar? God puts you in situations you are uncomfortable with, and rather than deal with them you run away and hide. You try to blend into the crowd and get lost. But God in His love will not allow you to hide. There is no escaping Him though you climb the highest mountain or dive into the deepest sea. A figurative serpent will be assigned to force you out to deal with it.

That is especially true regarding your sin. "Be sure your sin will find you out" (Numbers 32:23). However deep you may attempt to bury your sin God sees it with exacting clarity. If you will not deal with your sin God will deal with you by allowing you to experience the negative consequences of your sin. So return to Him before He must act.

Love without TRUTH is *permissiveness.*

For sin shall not [any longer] exert dominion over you,
since now you are not under Law [as slaves],
but under grace [as subjects of God's favor and mercy].
What then [are we to conclude]? Shall we sin because
we live not under Law but under God's favor and mercy?
Certainly not!

ROMANS 6:14, 15

IF YOUR FAITH is soft on issues of sin you need to realize that biblical truth has either been removed from it or perverted within it. In the wrong hands any truth can be twisted and perverted. There is no biblical truth, including the grace of God, that opens the door to permissiveness on sin. Grace teaches that God forgives sinners upon the basis of His mercy in the sacrifice of His Son Jesus, and everything in salvation flows from His grace. Intrinsic to salvation is the fact that you are set free from the habit and desire to sin. The blood of Christ cleanses you as well as forgives, and love for Jesus and love for purity is born into your life. Bring a soft heart to God that includes a hatred for sin.

Your flesh can't keep you happy,
so stop trying to keep it happy.
OBEY THE SPIRIT,
and the desires of the flesh *will die.*

And those who belong to Christ Jesus (the Messiah)
have crucified the flesh (the godless human
nature) with its passions and appetites and desires.
If we live by the [Holy] Spirit, let us also walk
by the Spirit. [If by the Holy Spirit we have
our life in God, let us go forward walking in line,
our conduct controlled by the Spirit.]

GALATIANS 5:24, 25

THE APOSTLE PAUL did not minimize the fact that the flesh with its passions and lusts will be a challenge to the believer. But he is adamant that you put to death the deeds of the flesh. To have received Jesus Christ by faith is the first gigantic step you take in doing that. You saw the evil in your own selfishness, and in repentance you moved to kill the flesh. Jesus Christ cannot come into your life as Lord without the crucifixion of sin. The fact that the flesh still troubles you does not change what has been done. The power of this new life is in the indwelling Holy Spirit. Live by His power and keep yourself walking in line with Him, and you will remain free from the self-life of the flesh, and Jesus will be formed in your character.

God formed us.
SATAN DEFORMED US.
Christ *transforms us.*

When Jesus had received the sour wine,
He said, It is finished!
And He bowed His head and gave up His spirit.

JOHN 19:30

TELL YOURSELF every day that "It is finished!" Tell it to yourself every time you think that through some obedience or sacrifice you are winning God's approval. Say it out loud when you begin to think your financial giving or your prayers or your Bible reading are in some measure meritorious. Take out the two-edged sword of God's Word and let "It is finished!" mean exactly what Jesus accomplished on Calvary.

On the cross, Jesus totally destroyed the power of Satan, sin, and death. His perfect obedience straight through to the cross rendered satisfaction to the justice of God, and your personal debt for sin was forgiven to the very last sin. Will you add something to the price Christ paid? There is nothing for you to add. The Spirit of God comes in a new and living way to take up His dwelling place in your heart and transform you from above. Let Him come and carry out what Christ has already accomplished for you.

Humility is a person
BELIEVING he can do nothing,
but God can do *all things*.

The Pharisee took his stand ostentatiously
and began to pray thus before and with himself:
God, I thank You that I am not like the rest
of men...or even like this tax collector here.
I fast twice a week; I give tithes of all that I gain.
But the tax collector, [merely] standing at a distance,
would not even lift up his eyes to heaven, but kept
striking his breast, saying, O God, be favorable
(be gracious, be merciful) to me,
the especially wicked sinner that I am!

LUKE 18:11–13

PRIDE IS ALWAYS evil because it declares a person's belief that he can get along without God. Pride is a person believing he can do anything on his own. Religious or spiritual pride, which is as common today as it was in the temple during Jesus' ministry, borders on blasphemy. In contrast, the tax collector exemplified the broken spirit and contrite heart that David said God will not despise (Psalm 51:17). To come before God as one poor in spirit is your only preparation for receiving the grace of God. Let humility open the door to the manifold mercies of God.

Many people who have been hurt
spend their whole *lives*
paying back or collecting debts.
THIS IS GOD'S JOB—*not yours.*

So shall you say to Joseph: Forgive (take up
and away all resentment and all claim to requital
concerning), I pray you now, the trespass of your brothers
and their sin, for they did evil to you. Now, we pray you,
forgive the trespass of the servants of your father's God.
And Joseph wept when they spoke thus to him.

GENESIS 50:17

IF ANYONE EVER had the right to feel bitter and vindictive toward others it was Joseph. His brothers hated him so badly they nearly murdered him but instead chose to sell him into slavery. He could have easily spent the following years in Egypt scheming on how he might pay his brothers back for their evil toward him should he get the chance. But if you read his story, there is never a hint of bitterness. Even when the opportunity came to punish his brothers he instead confessed his unwavering faith in the providence of God.

The psalmist David once prayed, "Vindicate me, O Lord, for I have walked in my integrity; I have [expectantly] trusted in, leaned on, and relied on the Lord without wavering and I shall not slide" (Psalm 26:1). Leave the getting even to God, and you'll have a heart free from bitterness.

A proud person tries to use God.
   A HUMBLE PERSON
allows God to *use him.*

*However, when Simon saw that the [Holy] Spirit
was imparted through the laying on of the apostles' hands,
he brought money and offered it to them,
saying, Grant me also this power and authority,
in order that anyone on whom I place
my hands may receive the Holy Spirit.*

ACTS 8:18, 19

WHETHER THE conversion of Simon the Sorcerer was genuine has long been a topic of speculation, but as a trained charlatan of considerable influence he was amazed by the miracles taking place and the power of the Holy Spirit that was imparted through John and Peter's laying on of hands. Seeing this as a means to increase his influence he offered the apostles money that he might receive this same power. It appeared to him that he could use God to make his trade even more profitable.

Faith rests upon the spiritual condition of humility, and humility is wrought in the heart by the gift of God's grace. Faith is an attitude of trust with humility, not an attitude of assurance with pride. Learn to humble yourself beneath God's hand, and be prepared to be used by God.

Mercy is your Father rescuing you
out of distressful situations
because of your RELATIONSHIP,
not your record.

Have mercy upon me, O God,
according to Your steadfast love;
according to the multitude of Your tender mercy
and loving-kindness blot out my transgressions.

PSALM 51:1

DAVID HID HIS murderous, adulterous relationship with Bathsheba for twelve long months before being confronted by Nathan's piercing words, "You are the man!" (2 Samuel 12:7). David's cry for mercy in Psalm 51 reflects the cry of one overwhelmed with guilt and the uncleanness of sin. All the remorse and brokenness that had been stored up in his soul broke loose with a cry for God's mercy. He offered no excuses for his sin, but appealed for mercy because there is no other appeal to make. Only the mercy of God could rescue him from the blood-stained iniquity of his soul.

Mercy is God's grace or loving-kindness in action toward man. It is love that is exercised toward the needy, especially toward those who have sinned. By definition mercy is never what you deserve. It is seen repeatedly in God's faithfulness to Israel despite the people's unfaithfulness. In the New Testament mercy is seen in the fulfillment of His promised kindness (Luke 1:54, 72) through the salvation brought to us by Christ (Titus 3:5, 6). Receive His mercy and rejoice in His salvation!

When *wrong* becomes right,
THE CONSCIENCE
has lost *its light*.

Woe to those who call evil good and good evil,
who put darkness for light and light for darkness,
who put bitter for sweet and sweet for bitter!
Woe to those who are wise in their own eyes and prudent
and shrewd in their own sight!

ISAIAH 5:20, 21

POSTMODERNISM fits well with the description in Isaiah 5. Postmoderns believe there is no absolute truth; truth is left for an individual or a group of individuals to decide. Relativism, the belief that truth is relative to the situation at hand, is applied by postmoderns to everything including issues of right and wrong.

Sounds very familiar to what the apostle Paul forecast for the end times: "Some will turn away from the faith, giving attention to deluding and seducing spirits and doctrines that demons teach, through the hypocrisy and pretensions of liars whose consciences are seared (cauterized)" (1 Timothy 4:1, 2). When the conscience, the faculty of the human spirit given to judge right and wrong, is seared, darkness reigns in the soul. Wrong will proudly be declared as right; immorality will be twisted into declarations of morality, and sin will be declared to be the healthy norm. Hold boldly to the truth of God's Word for it alone will save you.

Many people can't
RECEIVE FORGIVENESS
because they're too busy
trying to *achieve forgiveness.*

For it is by free grace (God's unmerited favor)
that you are saved (delivered from judgment and made
partakers of Christ's salvation) through [your] faith.
And this [salvation] is not of yourselves [of your
own doing, it came not through your own striving],
but it is the gift of God; not because of works
[not the fulfillment of the Law's demands],
lest any man should boast.

EPHESIANS 2:8, 9

YOU CAN TRY to work for your forgiveness until your dying breath, and you'll never come close to meriting it. If you consider your christening or confirmation or baptism or partaking of the Lord's Supper or doing specific good works as somehow earning your way to forgiveness, you'll find no biblical basis for it. Or if you are trying to achieve forgiveness through your feelings, you're grasping for the wind. You will never "feel forgiven" enough, and if you think you're getting close, those feelings will be gone tomorrow.

For grace to be grace you can't mix in works—period. Forgiveness is by grace—by the free favor of God's gift in Jesus Christ. The only means to forgiveness is to receive God's undeserved mercy by faith—both now and forever. Discover your worth in His finished work, not in your works.

Life Line #3: CHARACTER

Character

What you are
is a result of what you've done
where you've been.

RESULT

The great test of every CHRISTIAN
is not preaching what he's learned,
but living what he preaches.

Look well to yourself [to your own personality]
and to [your] teaching; persevere in these things
[hold to them], for by so doing you will save
both yourself and those who hear you.

1 TIMOTHY 4:16

PERHAPS YOU HAVE heard the story of the man who preached so well and lived so badly that when he was in the pulpit everyone said he should never come out again and when he was out of it they all agreed he should never enter it again. Unfortunately, this story is occasionally too close to the truth. It is dreadful to be an inconsistent Christian. How you live your life speaks louder than your words, and the sinful actions of your life not only negate your words but can be a terrible offense to the Gospel.

Do you trust people who say one thing but live another way? Your words are important but who you are and how you live is far more compelling. Our Lord puts more emphasis on holy character than words. True believers live like believers whether or not anyone is watching. Rest assured that our Lord is always watching.

Difficult situations are opportunities
FOR GOD TO DO
things to you or *through you.*

Consider it wholly joyful, my brethren, whenever
you are enveloped in or encounter trials of any sort
or fall into various temptations.
Be assured and understand that the trial
and proving of your faith bring out endurance
and steadfastness and patience.

JAMES 1:2, 3

IT IS NOT NATURAL for the human heart to consider trials and temptations as James suggests. How does one look upon pain and difficulty and muster up joy? It is impossible to make sense of this...unless you read the second sentence. It is not the trials or the temptations you find pleasure in but the fact that God is using these to work in your life in a way that yields the sweet treasures of endurance and steadfastness and patience.

The difficult lessons that life brings your way are the road to experience and maturity. If you are tested with fire it is that you might be tempered by the Spirit of God. The fire has a work to do that nothing else can ever effect. God has chosen these for your good that you might become complete in your faith. If you want to be blessed, learn to press through the test.

The authenticity of a person
IS SEEN when his exterior
truly reflects *his interior.*

Then Job arose and rent his robe and shaved his head
and fell down upon the ground and worshiped
and said...The Lord gave and the Lord has taken away;
blessed (praised and magnified in worship)
be the name of the Lord!

JOB 1:20, 21

JOB'S LIFE WAS marked by a reverence for God, prosperity, and affluence. But the day came for Job to be tested in a trial of his faith that nearly defies description—the loss of his children, his wealth, and his health. In a direct confrontation with Satan over the authenticity of his faith Job was brought to that moment that everyone must face—the revelation of their character. No one escapes being tested.

Job's interior life proved to be stronger than the external. When the trials broke like a storm upon him Job wisely went back to the basic truth upon which his spiritual life rested: "The Lord gave and the Lord has taken away; blessed (praised and magnified in worship) be the name of the Lord!" With everything stripped away from his life Job would not give up the only thing that ultimately mattered—his commitment to God and a holy character. Will your character stand up to the test?

God will honor you
IF YOU GO BEYOND
your feelings to obey Him.

Blessed (happy, fortunate, and to be envied) is the man
who reverently and worshipfully fears [the Lord]
at all times [regardless of circumstances],
but he who hardens his heart will fall into calamity.

PROVERBS 28:14

WHEREVER I GO I meet simple, often uneducated believers who possess a brokenness of heart and a deep reverence for God that have transformed their character. Invariably they have a wealth of wisdom and insight others seek out and are drawn to Christ by. Their humility and love for God are charming.

Reverence for the Lord is the foundation of your relationship with Him. Solomon began his Proverbs by saying, "The reverent and worshipful fear of the Lord is the beginning and the principal and choice part of knowledge" (Proverbs 1:7). Without reverence and a worshipful fear all the knowledge you gather about God and all the spiritual feelings you can possibly muster will amount to nothing. Reverent obedience from the depths of your heart is necessary to the building of godly character in your life as a foundation with solid cornerstones. Honor God by moving beyond feelings into obedience based on the fact that He is God Almighty and worthy of it.

The more *God's going to* do with you, THE MORE HE'S GOT *to deal* with you.

For the time being no discipline brings joy,
but seems grievous and painful; but afterwards it yields
a peaceable fruit of righteousness to those
who have been trained by it [a harvest of fruit
which consists in righteousness—in conformity
to God's will in purpose, thought, and action,
resulting in right living and right standing with God].

HEBREWS 12:11

THE HEBREW BELIEVERS were suffering persecution and were very discouraged. They were told to endure it as discipline from the Lord, as corrective and instructive training for their spiritual growth. If you are God's child you will realize the things that touch your life are administered by your Father in heaven. For the moment it is very painful, but it will ultimately yield a conformity to God's will in your life that you have never known before.

Remember it is God's will to shape your life into a precious vessel that brings glory to Him. You have a great need to live near to Him and let Him deal with you as your Father. Extraordinary service for God requires superior strength of grace and inner purity. Allow your Father to work that into your character by His discipline of your life.

Your future is determined by
WHAT IT IS
constructed of—what you say
or do *under pressure.*

*And let us not lose heart and grow weary and faint
in acting nobly and doing right,
for in due time and at the appointed season we shall reap,
if we do not loosen and relax our courage and faint.*

GALATIANS 6:9

STRESS IS A part of everyone's life. Pressure can wear you down and make you feel like throwing in the towel. The difficulties you face today and the anxieties that trouble you for the moment shape your life—positively or negatively, depending on how you respond to them. Adversity and pain will test your character and challenge your faith to grow deeper.

You don't really know yourself until the sky grows dark and the winds and storms break in upon you. Faith in Jesus Christ will sustain you through whatever God allows to come your way. Draw strength from His grace and comfort. Choose to rejoice in the Lord and ask Him to give you the light you need to walk with Him to the very end of the battle. When the pressure is on, press through.

Extended inactivity is disguised
PROCRASTINATION.
Obedience delayed is disobedience!

Samuel said, Has the Lord as great a delight
in burnt offerings and sacrifices as in obeying
the voice of the Lord? Behold, to obey is better
than sacrifice, and to hearken than the fat of rams.
For rebellion is as the sin of witchcraft,
and stubbornness is as idolatry.

1 SAMUEL 15:22, 23

IN GOING INTO battle with the Amalekites, Samuel's word to King Saul was to utterly destroy every person and animal. Amalek was under a curse, and the existence of the tribe was a menace to the surrounding nations (Exodus 17:16). Saul, however, spared the Amalekite king and the best of the animals. On top of that, Saul set up for himself a monument to his victory and told Samuel he had fully performed what the Lord ordered (1 Samuel 15:13). It was this partial obedience, regarded by God as disobedience of the worst sort, that caused God to reject Saul as king. It is also noteworthy that it was an Amalekite who later claimed to take Saul's life on the field of Gilboa (2 Samuel 1:1–10). If you spare what God has commanded to be destroyed, it may later destroy you. Take care to make your obedience full.

CHOICES

The choices once made
ARE OUR LIVES
we now live.

And He said to them, Come after Me
  [as disciples—letting Me be your Guide], follow Me,
    and I will make you fishers of men!
At once they left their nets and became His disciples
  [sided with His party and followed Him].

MATTHEW 4:19, 20

SIMON, ANDREW, JAMES, and John were all common fishermen who had attached themselves to Jesus as disciples. But Jesus' improbable call to leave their nets and follow Him involved a choice that would forever change their lives. To leave their livelihoods and families was to surrender all. That same voice of Jesus speaks to you to follow Him as His servant and soldier. How you respond to His call will forever shape your life as well.

Who would have thought that these ordinary men so skilled at handling their nets would be transformed by the Master of men into founders of the early church? And who can say what He will transform you into? If He can make a Galilean fisherman into an apostle, what can He make of you? The key is to surrender whatever the Lord asks from you and to obey His voice. Let Him free you from your sin by His grace and make you into a fisher of men.

Trials are gates
TO GO THROUGH
on the road *to success.*

[You should] be exceedingly glad on this account,
though now for a little while you may be distressed
by trials and suffer temptations,
so that [the genuineness] of your faith may be tested,
[your faith] which is infinitely more precious
than the perishable gold which is tested
and purified by fire. [This proving of your faith
is intended] to redound to [your] praise and glory
and honor when Jesus Christ (the Messiah,
the Anointed One) is revealed.

1 PETER 1:6, 7

THE BRETHREN TO whom Peter was writing were truly suffering as Christians. Falsely maligned, they stood before pagan judges who confiscated their property, scourged and tortured them, imprisoned some, and sentenced some to death in the arena or by fire. These trials were meant to test, purify, and strengthen their faith that no matter how difficult the situation their lives might give praise and glory to Jesus.

Too often you try to engineer your way out of the trials you face. Rather than wait upon God to help you through, you distrust Him and look for a way of escape. And each time you run, your faith is weakened. Rather, see trials as God's gates on the way to successful growth in your faith.

Many Christians want God to
GIVE THEM PEACE
in the midst of what they want to do,
despite what God has *told them to do.*

Will the Lord be pleased with thousands of rams
or with ten thousands of rivers of oil?
Shall I give my firstborn for my transgression,
the fruit of my body for the sin of my soul?
He has showed you, O man, what is good.
And what does the Lord require of you but to do justly,
and to love kindness and mercy, and to humble yourself
and walk humbly with your God?

MICAH 6:7, 8

HOW HYPOCRITICAL are believers when they try to play spiritual games with God? You know the routine. You want to have His gift of peace, but you choose to disregard what He has already shown you. You even make sacrifices to God to cover over your hypocrisy and disobedience, as if they might bring Him pleasure. The Lord cuts through the game playing and says, "Stop it! Keep your sacrifices to yourself. It's all wrong and you have forced me to turn away. There is one thing I desire: Do what I have shown you to do. Obey what I have said. Submit to Me with all your heart, and then I will give you a peace that surpasses understanding."

A *strong Christian* is one who does
THE RIGHT THING
under the wrong *circumstances.*

Then after a time his master's wife
cast her eyes upon Joseph, and she said, Lie with me.
But he refused and said to his master's wife...
How then can I do this great evil and sin against God?

GENESIS 39:7–9

BEFORE JOSEPH FOUND himself in a moral crisis as a slave in the house of Potiphar, he passed through abuse and suffering and his integrity had remained in God. When this great temptation broke in upon the young man, consider his situation. As a slave he had no real future outside the household. Besides the immediate sexual attraction and his own loneliness, if he captured her affections and played it to his advantage perhaps it was an opportunity for freedom. And if he refused her repeated advances, would he fare worse than if he took advantage?

Wrong circumstances such as these can blast into your life without warning. When the temptation steps in your path, what is your response? Joseph's response was to flee to God. Temptations loom before us every day and there is only one answer that conquers all—God! Establish the integrity of your heart in Jesus Christ or you will have no power to overcome temptation.

Does *opposition*
STIR YOU UP
or *shut you up?*

And now, Lord, observe their threats and grant
to Your bond servants [full freedom] to declare
Your message fearlessly, while You stretch out
Your hand to cure and to perform signs and wonders
through the authority and by the power of the name
of Your holy Child and Servant Jesus.
And when they had prayed, the place in which
they were assembled was shaken; and they were all filled
with the Holy Spirit, and they continued to speak
the Word of God with freedom and boldness and courage.

ACTS 4:29–31

THE APOSTLES HAD been threatened to not speak or teach at all in the name of Jesus by the same religious leaders who had sentenced Jesus to death, but the apostles issued an immediate refusal (Acts 4:19, 20). It was impossible to not speak of the Savior. Furthermore, when they repeated the story to the church that also stood at risk of persecution, rather than be silenced they joined together in a glorious prayer to declare His name fearlessly! And though they had been filled with the Holy Spirit before, they were filled again. Let opposition to the gospel stir you up to stand with the Spirit no matter what the consequences may be.

If you don't learn
HOW TO DEAL with trouble,
trouble will deal with you.

He who guards his mouth
and his tongue
keeps himself from troubles.

IF YOU ARE FAMILIAR with the biblical story of Jonah you realize his experience is not unlike your own. The Lord speaks to your heart, puts His finger on an area of your life He wants to change, and rather than respond in loving obedience you head straight in the opposite direction (Jonah 1:3). God's assignment is not to your liking and you don't want the trouble.

But there is no escape from God and you always pay the price when you go your own way. He speaks to the wind and in no time the trouble faced upon the seas is far more difficult than the troubles that might be faced in obedience. God can make all things work to do His will and it is far easier to deal with trouble than to have God bring trouble to you. After the winds there's a specially prepared fish that all the complaining in the world will not eliminate. Complaining only keeps you nailed to your problems. Say yes to God in the first place and you'll keep yourself from a sea of trouble.

Life Lines / MEYER / 68

The cutting edge of God
IN YOUR LIFE
can become dull
if you resist His *chastening love.*

My son, do not despise or shrink from the chastening
of the Lord [His correction by punishment
or by subjection to suffering or trial];
neither be weary of or impatient about or loathe
or abhor His reproof, for whom the Lord loves
He corrects, even as a father corrects the son
in whom he delights.

PROVERBS 3:11, 12

YOUR FATHER IN heaven shapes your character through suffering and trials and divine correction. Just as the refiner sits over the glowing furnace and the sculptor employs the sharp chisel, so your Father chastens and disciplines you through His love that you might bear the image of His Son. To despise or shrink from His hand is to miss His purpose completely and actually lose the cutting edge of God in your life. Rather than be patient and allow it to sanctify and perfect you, you try to escape the pruning shears. Solomon says to look beyond the suffering or the sorrow and see the One behind it. While you may not understand its purpose, you can rest in the assurance that your Father wants you to share in His holiness.

You can never be a *"lesser than"*
    unless you are intimidated
by someone you think is
    A "MORE THAN."
You can't be excluded
if you don't need to *be included.*

But when Cephas (Peter) came to Antioch,
I protested and opposed him to his face
    [concerning his conduct there], for he was
blameable and stood condemned.

IT IS IMPORTANT that you read the entire account of the apostle Paul's confrontation of the apostle Peter (Galatians 2:11–21). Paul could have easily been intimidated by Peter, who had spent over three years with Christ and was recognized as the leader of the early church. But when Peter withdrew his fellowship from Gentile believers because of fear and fractured the unity of the church in Antioch, Paul confronted Peter immediately on the basis of truth, sincerity, and conviction. Regardless of Peter's ranking in the leadership of the church, Paul would not succumb to Peter's hypocrisy and the fact that his fellow Jews had also separated from the Gentiles. Better to stand alone with Christ and truth than to stand on condemned ground with apostles.

Determination
OPENS THE DOOR
for extermination of *procrastination.*

And Ruth said, Urge me not to leave you
or to turn back from following you; for where you go
I will go, and where you lodge I will lodge.
Your people shall be my people and your God my God.
When Naomi saw that Ruth was determined
to go with her, she said no more.

RUTH 1:16, 18

AS A MOABITE and a young widow Ruth had good reasons to not go with Naomi back to Judah. But she had come to love her mother-in-law deeply and had put her faith in Naomi's God. Out of that passionate love Ruth determined that any sacrifice she had to make was worth it. It is not surprising that this woman with such a great heart was grafted into the actual lineage of Christ's descent through King David.

How much more should your love for Jesus Christ be driven by a determination to follow Him without hesitation to the ends of the earth. Determination is an attitude, not a feeling. You must decide—not wait—to be moved.

It's easy to give people
WHAT THEY DESERVE,
but it's a privilege to *give them mercy*.

Blessed (happy, to be envied,
and spiritually prosperous—with life-joy and satisfaction
in God's favor and salvation, regardless
of their outward conditions) are the merciful,
for they shall obtain mercy!

MATTHEW 5:7

IF YOU READ the short book of Philemon you realize Paul's concern in sending Onesimus back to Philemon. Onesimus was a slave of Philemon who had run away. Philemon had a legal right to punish him. Philemon had been wronged. Is it natural to be merciful in such a situation? Was it not appropriate to assert his mastery over his slave? Paul asks Philemon to be merciful and to receive him as a forgiven brother in the Lord.

It is a marvelous privilege to be merciful and reflect to others the mercy God has given to you. To have the Spirit of Christ dwelling inside you is to have inherent mercy shaping your character. Mercy is another name for love—love with tears, love with pity. Mercy has no scale or time clock to measure out love. Mercy is a hand stretched out and a word in season. May mercy be the perpetual blessedness reigning in your soul.

Learn to live by the
PRESENCE OF THE LORD,
not by the *presents of the Lord.*

Though the fig tree does not blossom
    and there is no fruit on the vines, [though] the product
        of the olive fails and the fields yield no food,
    though the flock is cut off from the fold
        and there are no cattle in the stalls,
    yet I will rejoice in the Lord;
I will exult in the [victorious] God of my salvation!

HABAKKUK 3:17, 18

YOU ARE GREATLY mistaken if you try to live your life on the basis of the presents of the Lord. Read through the Book of Habakkuk and you discover a troubled prophet caught in a dark period perplexed by what God was doing and not doing. Habakkuk was not afraid to detail his specific questions to God and when the answer came, it boiled down to this principle: A believer must live by simple faith in God.

There are periods of your Christian life when the Lord remains silent and asks you to wait on Him. Even if all of God's gifts seem to fail, the abiding presence of the Lord cannot be taken from you. You still belong to the Giver and He belongs to you. Rejoice in Him as your God no matter what your circumstances.

Responsibility is one's
ABILITY TO RESPOND
without being fond of what one is
responsible for.

His master said to him, Well done, you upright
(honorable, admirable) and faithful servant!
You have been faithful and trustworthy over a little;
I will put you in charge of much. Enter into
and share the joy (the delight, the blessedness)
which your master enjoys.

MATTHEW 25:21

AS A SERVANT of God, you have been given gifts and talents from Him to use for His kingdom and glory. While others may have far greater talents than yours, you have at least one gift for which you are responsible to give an account to God. It is a principle within God's kingdom that as you are faithful and responsible to what God has given you He will advance you to a higher service. Being faithful where you are and with what God has given you to do now has nothing to do with whether you are particularly fond of what that responsibility entails.

Two aspects of your responsibility stand out in Matthew 25. First, there is a day coming when you shall give an account for your faithfulness to what God gave you to do. And, second, if you are faithful your divine Master offers that you may enter His joy is beyond description. "Enter in," Jesus says, "and share the joy!"

For you to move on
   to a higher level *with God,*
YOU MUST PASS
   the test at *the level you are.*

Yes, furthermore, I count everything as loss
   compared to the possession of the priceless privilege
(the overwhelming preciousness, the surpassing
   worth, and supreme advantage) of knowing Christ
Jesus my Lord and of progressively becoming
   more deeply and intimately acquainted with Him
[of perceiving and recognizing and understanding Him
   more fully and clearly]. For His sake I have lost
everything and consider it all to be mere rubbish
   (refuse, dregs), in order that I may win
   (gain) Christ (the Anointed One).

           PHILIPPIANS 3:8

THE APOSTLE PAUL'S greatest joy was to know Jesus Christ as God's gift, but he was not content with this. Paul passionately desired to win or gain Christ—to know Him and the power of His resurrection and the fellowship of His sufferings. To do that he surrendered himself completely to God's service and welcomed whatever it might cost him personally.

  The quality of your commitment to Christ is reflected in the cost you are willing to bear. May there be no reservation in your commitment. Give yourself wholly to Him, and the pearl of great price you receive will far exceed the costs!

Success is the result of
PASSING TESTS
where you chose to do the best
with the option *to do less.*

I have fought the good (worthy, honorable,
and noble) fight, I have finished the race,
I have kept (firmly held) the faith. [As to what
remains] henceforth there is laid up for me
the [victor's] crown of righteousness [for being
right with God and doing right], which the Lord,
the righteous Judge, will award to me
and recompense me on that [great] day—and not
to me only, but also to all those who have loved
and yearned for and welcomed
His appearing (His return).

2 TIMOTHY 4:7, 8

PAUL LEFT TIMOTHY with his profound legacy for a truly successful life—fighting the good fight, finishing the race, and firmly holding to the faith in Jesus Christ. It's not just for apostles; it's for every believer. Is it costly? Certainly. It cost Paul everything. But he endured for the victor's crown Jesus had for him…and for every believer.

To run the race you must feed on God's Word for strength and meet the challenges you face—one at a time. The prize in being a winner is found in the price of becoming a winner.

It is easy to be
LONGSUFFERING
with someone if you have
suffered long in the *same areas.*

I therefore, the prisoner of the Lord, beseech you
that ye walk worthy of the vocation wherewith ye are
called, with all lowliness and meekness,
with longsuffering, forbearing one another in love.

EPHESIANS 4:1, 2 KJV

THANK GOD THAT He is "long-suffering and slow to anger, and abundant in mercy and loving-kindness, forgiving iniquity and transgression" (Numbers 14:18). To be longsuffering is to literally be "long tempered," which God has graciously been with you even when you were at your very worst. This is the way you are to be toward others even when they are at their worst.

Through the Holy Spirit this very quality of God is meant to be reproduced in your life, and it involves putting your own selfishness to death (Galatians 5:22). Death to the flesh equals a willingness to hurt until hope is fulfilled. It means to have the power of self-restraint in the face of provocation. Refuse to surrender to circumstances but remain patient with others and never lose hope for them (Nehemiah 9:17).

Life Line #4:
LIFE in CHRIST

Nothing can be done through
a Christian *unless* he has
FIRST ALLOWED GOD
to *work humility* in him.

Don't be afraid of the darkness
in the earth today.
REMEMBER THIS:
Light shines best in darkness.

Let your light so shine before men
that they may see your moral excellence
and your praiseworthy, noble, and good deeds
and recognize and honor and praise and glorify
your Father Who is in heaven.

MATTHEW 5:16

IT IS THE NATURE of light to shine, and the darker the night the brighter the light. There is darkness in the world, and moral darkness is the blackest of all. Perhaps where you live today has become a very dark place, a fearful place. Perhaps the light has been so obscured you are tempted to think there is no light at all, only darkness.

The purpose of God is that you shine and illuminate the world in which you live. There is no light and no life but that of Jesus Christ (John 1:4). What He is in Himself is what He gives to you. Never be content until your life is fully illumined by Christ. By the beauty of holiness reflected in your life the darkness will be driven back. If you live your Christianity, the light in your life will flood the darkness with the true glory of God.

God knew what you would be
      BEFORE YOU BECAME,
because *He saw* who you were
      while you were *still becoming.*

Faithful is He Who is calling you [to Himself]
      and utterly trustworthy, and He will also do it
   [fulfill His call by hallowing and keeping you].

1 THESSALONIANS 5:24

OUR GOD IS utterly faithful. If you are a believer in Jesus Christ you are a beloved child of God. Your calling to salvation and sanctification are rooted in God's eternal love for you, and His purposes are being worked out daily in your life through the power of the Holy Spirit. Has He ever failed you? Has He forgotten you? Has He not kept every promise He has made to you in His Word? Is there any reason to believe that He who began a good work in you will not bring it to completion?

No matter what you face, God is faithful. He will never fail anyone who dares to be all that He wills. Because He is faithful He will stand by you to the end. He will never do anything less than what He has promised. He will never draw back from the covenant of love He has given you, so put the full weight of your faith in Him alone.

If you will not run
when you feel fear,
FEAR WILL RUN
because it has *seen faith.*

And do not [for a moment] be frightened
or intimidated in anything by your opponents
and adversaries, for such [constancy and fearlessness]
will be a clear sign (proof and seal) to them
of [their impending] destruction, but [a sure token
and evidence] of your deliverance and salvation,
and that from God.

PHILIPPIANS 1:28

IT IS A GREAT mistake to think that coming into the kingdom of God involves an easy ride to heaven. For the believers in Philippi it meant real hostility and persecution. Jesus never said you would be greeted with honor and cheers. Jesus called you to bear your own cross, which is a miniature copy of the cross that He bore for you.

Jesus said you are to consider yourself "blessed" when you are persecuted for righteousness' sake, for the kingdom of heaven is yours (Matthew 5:10). That remains true. To live a godly life in a world of darkness will not win you a popularity contest. Never be frightened or intimidated by the world's hatred. Rather, take it as a joy to suffer for Jesus and let your light shine without fear as a witness to the world.

A *position* of power
can be obtained IN YOUR LIFE
when you learn to be encouraged
in a *discouraging* situation.

Then he was afraid and arose and went
for his life...a day's journey into the wilderness
and came and sat down under a lone broom or
juniper tree and asked that he might die.
He said, It is enough; now, O Lord, take away my life.

1 KINGS 19:3, 4

ELIJAH HAD JUST seen the fire fall from heaven in answer to prayer, the priests of Baal had been slaughtered, and the rain had deluged the barren land as he had spoken. But at the height of victory Elijah fell into an overwhelming depression that was prompted by fear for his life. Exhausted and broken he fled from Jezebel and hid in the seclusion of the wilderness and asked the Lord to take his life. Elijah pushed past being on the cutting edge for God and found himself on the ragged edge of collapse. God sent the angel of the Lord to strengthen Elijah and led him forward to a divine encounter that lifted Elijah to a place of power he had not known before (1 Kings 19:7–18).

Every believer goes through times of discouragement. Pray honestly to God and He will strengthen you and meet you where you are.

All Christians love growth
IN THE SPIRIT,
but many don't love *growing.*
Remember, the formula for growth
is a *period of growing.*

I assure you, most solemnly I tell you,
   Unless a grain of wheat falls into the earth and dies,
it remains [just one grain; it never becomes more
      but lives] by itself alone. But if it dies, it produces
      many others and yields a rich harvest.
Anyone who loves his life loses it, but anyone who hates
   his life in this world will keep it to life eternal.

JOHN 12:24, 25

THE CHRISTIAN LIFE is a bit of a paradox. Salvation and all you receive comes from God's grace—period. There is absolutely nothing you can bring to purchase your salvation. But to be a disciple of Jesus means He must be first in everything in your life. Spiritual growth comes out of your life falling like a grain of wheat into the earth and dying—a very real death to the flesh. Wherever your own pleasure, gain, honor, or interest comes before Christ it must be put to death with its desires and lusts that the life of Jesus might be everything. The cost, however painful it may feel, is unavoidable that your spirit might be free to enjoy all Jesus has for you.

God's waiting for you.
COME AS YOU ARE,
not as you're trying to become.
He'll make you what you *are to be.*

Come to Me, all you who labor and are heavy-laden
and overburdened, and I will cause you to rest.
[I will ease and relieve and refresh your souls.]
Take My yoke upon you and learn of Me, for I am
gentle (meek) and humble (lowly) in heart,
and you will find rest (relief and ease and refreshment
and recreation and blessed quiet) for your souls.

MATTHEW 11:28, 29

DO YOU HEAR the sweet tone of the Savior's call to "Come to Me"? Why do you make Him wait? He knows exactly what you are going through and exactly what you need. He is not asking you to first become qualified to come before Him. He is asking only that you come as a child before Him. His way is for you to take upon yourself His yoke and to learn from Him. He will reveal His heart to you and you will find the rest you need for your soul. To walk in the same yoke with Jesus is to have your life transformed by His presence. It means to bow in submission to the Father's loving will and to walk step by step with Jesus. There is no better place you can possibly be than that!

If you put your schedule
BEFORE GOD,
the devil will make sure
He doesn't have *a place.*

But the Lord replied to her by saying,
Martha, Martha, you are anxious and troubled
about many things; there is need of only one or
but a few things. Mary has chosen the good portion
[that which is to her advantage],
which shall not be taken away from her.

LUKE 10:41, 42

MARTHA, NOT UNLIKE you and me, had an agenda to accomplish. While Mary sat at the feet of Jesus listening to His every word, Martha was overly occupied with much serving. She had put her schedule before Jesus and she was about to let her frustration boil over and miss the blessing of the Lord's presence. It is easy to understand the bitterness of her complaint: "Lord, is it nothing to You that my sister has left me to serve alone? Tell her then to help me [to lend a hand and do her part along with me]!" (Luke 10:40).

Jesus gently showed Martha that her first priority needed to be built around Him, despite the needs of the household that seemed so pressing at the moment. To sit at the feet of Jesus was a feast from which she must first partake. If you work your schedule around God everything else will fall into place.

While you are *waiting to get*
WHERE YOU ARE GOING,
you must learn to *enjoy where you are.*

I know how to be abased and live humbly
   in straitened circumstances, and I know also
how to enjoy plenty and live in abundance.
I have learned in any and all circumstances
   the secret of facing every situation, whether well-fed
or going hungry, having a sufficiency and enough
   to spare or going without and being in want.

PHILIPPIANS 4:12

THE APOSTLE PAUL spoke these remarkable words while he was in jail awaiting a trial that could mean his death. Learning to be content, to enjoy where you are in life no matter what your circumstances, is a secret unlocked by growth through experience in living in the will of God. Paul knew that as long as his life was in God's hand nothing could change that, and that was the best possible place he could be.

Contentment must be learned, especially in a culture that worships at the altar of climbing the ever-elusive ladder of success. For most people contentment in the face of competition and sacrifice to get ahead is but a distant memory of the kindergarten years. It can be rediscovered through Christ. If everything in your life centers on Christ—including your ambitions and circumstances— you have everything you need, and no one can take that away.

Tomorrow may not come,
and YESTERDAY IS PAST.
Live each day as though it is your last.

Come now, you who say, Today or tomorrow
we will go into such and such a city and spend
a year there and carry on our business
and make money. Yet you do not know
[the least thing] about what may happen tomorrow.
What is the nature of your life? You are [really]
but a wisp of vapor (a puff of smoke, a mist) that is visible
for a little while and then disappears [into thin air].

JAMES 4:13, 14

LIFE IS FAR MORE uncertain and fragile than we like to imagine it. When we leave home in the morning there is no guarantee we will return in the evening. The mortal reality is that when we say good-bye, it might be final. Tomorrow does not always come.

Paul brought a wonderfully simple perspective to living: "For me to live is Christ [His life in me], and to die is gain [the gain of the glory of eternity]" (Philippians 1:21). If living day by day is simply "Christ," if Christ "is our life" (Colossians 3:4), if His will is your will today, you live as though it is your last. And if it is, what difference does it make? Death is but a gain of glory. How sweet will that be?

You must be willing
TO SACRIFICE,
but not to *compromise.*

*I appeal to you therefore, brethren, and beg of you
in view of [all] the mercies of God, to make
a decisive dedication of your bodies [presenting all your
members and faculties] as a living sacrifice,
holy (devoted, consecrated) and well pleasing
to God, which is your reasonable (rational, intelligent)
service and spiritual worship.*

ROMANS 12:1

THE CHRISTIAN LIFE is characterized by sacrifice. It begins with a surrender of your will to the lordship of Christ because He is worthy of all your life, and it continues with the daily surrender of your life because He is worthy. You are a living sacrifice totally dedicated to using your talents and gifts to bring worship and praise to your loving Father.

But Paul reminds you the world is not your friend. "Do not be conformed to this world (this age), [fashioned after and adapted to its external, superficial customs], but be transformed (changed) by the [entire] renewal of your mind [by its new ideals and its new attitude]" (Romans 12:2). You must be transformed by a mind that is renewed, made new like the morning, made strong with an energy that cannot be exhausted. Why? Because it is the only way to prove, test and know the will of God, and then to find out the best way of accomplishing it.

To be able *to love people*
      when they are unlovely,
you must *learn* to
      RECEIVE GOD'S LOVE
when you have *acted unlovely.*

Above all things have intense and unfailing love
   for one another, for love covers a multitude of sins
[forgives and disregards the offenses of others].

1 PETER 4:8

PETER WAS AN apostle who knew well the meaning of the words, "love covers a multitude of sins." Peter received three specific warnings from Jesus Christ and yet he denied his Lord three times. The memory of each painful failure was etched across his heart with untold grief. Surely he was not worthy of the Lord's kingdom. And yet when Christ arose, His love for Peter was unbroken. His love was as strong as it was tender in restoring the fallen apostle.

The capacity to love those who are unlovely begins with the understanding that God loved you when you were as unlovely as you could possibly be. "But God shows and clearly proves His [own] love for us by the fact that while we were still sinners, Christ (the Messiah, the Anointed One) died for us" (Romans 5:8). With the love of God poured out in your heart (vs. 5) transforming you disregard the offenses of others.

The devil cannot get a
STRONGHOLD
unless you give him *a foothold.*

For the weapons of our warfare are not
physical [weapons of flesh and blood],
but they are mighty before God for the overthrow
and destruction of strongholds, [inasmuch as
we] refute arguments and theories and reasonings
and every proud and lofty thing that sets itself up
against the [true] knowledge of God; and we lead
every thought and purpose away captive into the obedience
of Christ (the Messiah, the Anointed One).

2 CORINTHIANS 10:4, 5

THE CHRISTIAN LIFE is warfare and much of the battle takes place inside your life. If you do not allow the enemy a foothold in your life he cannot establish a stronghold. You have a supernatural arsenal at your disposal that is mighty through God because God is in you. It begins by establishing a genuine prayer life where you commune with your Father in heaven. This is the power engine of the battle. It is strengthened by daily feedings on the Word of God, the sword of the Spirit. Truth and holiness at work in your life overthrow and destroy the enemy's work.

Allow the Gospel to come into your daily life with the power of the Holy Spirit and you will be armed for the fight and victorious in the battle.

If you want to be led
BY THE SPIRIT,
don't hurry *or worry.*

May the God of your hope so fill you with all joy
and peace in believing [through the experience
of your faith] that by the power of the Holy
Spirit you may abound and be overflowing
(bubbling over) with hope.

ROMANS 15:13

IF YOU ARE constantly troubled and anxious and fretting and running around in an attempt to hold your life together, you are not being led by the Spirit. You were called to the peace of God that the Spirit of peace might be shed abroad and rule in your heart. It begins with being at peace with God, having a heart settled in the knowledge your sins are forgiven and cleansed. Then it extends to being at peace with the will of God. You no longer quarrel with God over what He has allowed to come into your life. You rest in His love and His purpose. And God's Spirit comes in and transforms your nature that has been twisted and corroded by sin, bringing peace where contention ruled. The peace of the Spirit will bring calm and quiet to your spirit and lead you on a course marked by peace.

If Jesus is going to live in you,
He is going to live
on HIS TERMS, *not yours.*

Jesus answered him, If you would be perfect [that is,
have that spiritual maturity which accompanies
self-sacrificing character], go and sell what you have
and give to the poor, and you will have
riches in heaven; and come, be My disciple
[side with My party and follow Me].

MATTHEW 19:21

THE RICH YOUNG ruler sincerely felt he had kept the stan-dards of the Law, not realizing he had failed to allow the Law to do its primary work—to convict him of sin. He had never seen the selfishness of his own heart until he pressed Jesus for a clear state-ment of what he lacked in order to inherit eternal life. Jesus knew the young man's heart was in slavery to his material possessions, and He directed His terms to the point of bondage. Jesus unmasked the selfishness of the young man's heart and allowed him to walk away "sad." Confronted with the choice of worshiping his great possessions or following Jesus he fades away to the synagogue where he can rule without breaking with the bondage in his life.

The Scottish writer George MacDonald said, "A man is in bondage to whatever he cannot part with that is less than himself." Jesus asks you to let go of everything that He might be yours.

God's manifest presence with you
IS A RESULT
of your manifest *presence with Him.*

If you live in Me [abide vitally united to Me]
and My words remain in you and continue to
live in your hearts, ask whatever you will,
and it shall be done for you.

JOHN 15:7

GOD'S MANIFOLD blessings, of which His presence with you is easily the greatest, come to you as you abide in your relationship with Jesus. Indeed Jesus made it clear that apart from Him you can do nothing (John 15:5). To "live in Me" means to be vitally one with Jesus, to enjoy all that it means to be in Christ. Prayer is a natural expression of a heart that is abiding in Christ—it is on your lips when you awake in the morning and flows naturally from you throughout your day. To live in His presence, to be in communion with Christ, is to know joy unspeakable and full of glory! You'll never receive any of God's blessings if you don't spend any of your time with God.

Satan wants you
TO BE ACTIVE
in things you can't do *anything about*
and *passive* in things you can.

*But to man He said, Behold, the reverential
and worshipful fear of the Lord—that is Wisdom;
and to depart from evil is understanding.*

JOB 28:28

KEEP IN MIND that if Christ were not in your life the devil would not bother with you. And the more united you are to Christ in spirit, the more you abide in Him, the more opposition you should expect. The next time Satan knocks on your door let Jesus answer his accusations. The sheep are always safe from the wolf when the Good Shepherd is near. Jesus is your righteousness, holiness, and redemption. He is your peace and He is your joy. If the devil reminds you of your sins and failures, the name of Jesus and His blood will drive him away. Whatever Satan's accusation do not allow him to get you to try to do something Jesus has already accomplished for you. Listen to Jesus and do the things He asks you to do.

He who chooses the road that
LEADS TO REWARD
will be accompanied by the
companions of *Obedience and Suffering.*

Although He was a Son, He learned [active, special]
obedience through what He suffered and,
[His completed experience] making Him perfectly
[equipped], He became the Author and
Source of eternal salvation to all those
who give heed and obey Him.

HEBREWS 5:8, 9

THE APOSTLE PAUL tells us concerning the life of Christ: "After He had appeared in human form, He abased and humbled Himself [still further] and carried His obedience to the extreme of death, even the death of the cross! Therefore [because He stooped so low] God has highly exalted Him" (Philippians 2:8, 9). Amazingly, our Lord as a man had to learn obedience and through suffering that led to His death. And through that obedience and suffering He was perfected as to His humanity.

If the Master walked this path that led to eternal reward, how much more you and I? You are learning to obey with Christ at your side. He knows the way, having walked it Himself. Surely you can trust Him to help you no matter where your obedience leads you. The reward is found in your faithfulness to the promises of God, not the enjoyments along the road.

You must learn to
MAINTAIN YOUR JOY
in the midst of the storm,
or the storm *will remain.*

And when the disciples saw Him walking on the sea,
they were terrified and said, It is a ghost!
And they screamed out with fright.
But instantly He spoke to them, saying,
Take courage! I AM! Stop being afraid!

MATTHEW 14:26, 27

THE DISCIPLES STRUGGLED for hours in the dark but could not beat the storm that threatened to take their boat down. How true that is to your own life experience. You struggle so hard with your work and problems that you lose your joy and peace. Yet if you look up through the waves of problems you find Christ walking straight over them to save you.

The storm will pass if you take Him into your boat. Your peace will not give way if it is centered in Him. Indeed peace is not peace unless it remains in the midst of the storm. God promises to "fill you with all joy and peace in believing [through the experience of your faith]" (Romans 15:13). The night may be dark and the waves real but Christ is greater than the storm.

God is more interested in
YOUR STABILITY
than your *tranquility.*

But his delight and desire are in the law of the Lord,
and on His law (the precepts, the instructions,
the teachings of God) he habitually meditates
(ponders and studies) by day and by night.
And he shall be like a tree firmly planted [and tended] by
the streams of water, ready to bring forth its fruit
in its season; its leaf also shall not fade or wither;
and everything he does shall prosper
[and come to maturity].

PSALM 1:2, 3

A LIFE ROOTED in God and His Word is like a tree rooted in the eternal stream. As long as the river runs and the quality of the water is good the tree will grow slowly and solidly, unlike the flower that shoots up quickly and is ever so fragile. Although the branches of the tree may creak and bend in the storm the roots are held firmly in divine soil.

As regards your life in the Spirit there is never a famine but always an abundance of fruit in season. Because your faith is in Jesus Christ the solid growth of your character is followed by solid actions that lead to prosperity and maturity. It is better to grow solid slowly than fragile quickly.

When making *a decision,*
after checking with your *head*
LOOK INTO YOUR HEART.
If you see peace, go ahead.

*And let the peace (soul harmony which comes) from
Christ rule (act as umpire continually) in your
hearts [deciding and settling with finality all
questions that arise in your minds, in that
peaceful state] to which as [members of Christ's]
one body you were also called [to live]. And be
thankful (appreciative), [giving praise to God always].*

COLOSSIANS 3:15

IN THE DAYS OF the apostle Paul, the Greek games were ruled by umpires whose word and verdict were final. An umpire's declaration of the breaking of a rule or of the victor ended any debate that might be involved in an event. So too, the peace that comes from your relationship with Jesus Christ is to rule your hearts in all matters. This inner peace is an assured quietness of soul, a calmness of spirit that stands up to the turmoil of life. Whenever you make decisions, if you think it is a good idea to go ahead you also need to let your heart speak. If you do not sense an inner peace from Christ you should not move ahead. Always be at peace with Christ in your heart and you will be able to meet life with joy and a quiet trust that overcomes.

Life Line #5:

SECRETS
of DAILY LIVING

You cannot stand still
       or you will stagnate;
YOU MUST GROW ON
       with the Lord. This means
you will need to grow up
              if you *want to go on.*

The *fear of the Lord* is to
KNOW GOD
as a *just* God.

The reverent, worshipful fear of the Lord leads to life,
and he who has it rests satisfied;
he cannot be visited with [actual] evil.

PROVERBS 19:23

"THE FEAR OF the Lord" is not the fear of someone crouching in a corner hoping that a tyrant won't see and punish them. The fear of the Lord Solomon describes is a sense of awe and reverence that comes from being exposed to the majesty and grandeur of God. The person who fears the Lord has moved beyond the intellectual acknowledgment of the attributes of God and recognizes that God in His Person stands for truth, purity, holiness, and justice.

To know in the depths of your heart that God is ultimate justice is to find life and hope and confidence. It is to know that God will reveal Himself and His will to you so clearly that you will know it is the true way. It is to know He is always doing the right thing in your life despite whatever adversity or twists and turns come into your life. What a blessing to know that your life is in God and that He is your refuge when the storms of life howl around you!

Are you impressed by
your circumstances or by
THE WORD OF GOD?
Whichever you choose determines
whether you *walk in faith or fear.*

And Mary said to the angel, How can this be,
since I have no [intimacy with any man as a]
husband? Then the angel said to her,
The Holy Spirit will come upon you,
and the power of the Most High will
overshadow you [like a shining cloud];
and so the holy (pure, sinless) Thing (Offspring)
which shall be born of you will be called the Son of God.

LUKE 1:34, 35

FEW PEOPLE IN the history of the world have ever faced more
impossible circumstances than Mary, the mother of Jesus. Imagine
a lone teenage girl who has just been told she will become preg-
nant by the Holy Spirit and that her child will be the Son of God.
No wonder the angel added, "For with God nothing is ever impossible and no word from God shall be without power or impossible
of fulfillment" (Luke 1:37). Yet Mary responded, "Let it be done to
me according to what you have said" (vs. 38). Her response was
full of faith that overcame any fear she may have been feeling.
Circumstances fade to the background whenever you hold God's
Word as supreme.

Many have not learned to hear
GOD'S VOICE
because they act *in the flesh*
when not knowing what to do,
instead of *waiting on God.*

*Saul waited seven days, according to the set time
Samuel had appointed. But Samuel had not come
to Gilgal, and the people were scattering from Saul.
So Saul said, Bring me the burnt offering and the peace
offerings. And he offered the burnt offering
[which he was forbidden to do]. And just as he finished
offering the burnt offering, behold, Samuel came!*

1 SAMUEL 13:8–10

DESPITE THE FACT he was facing an overwhelming force of
Philistines and his own troops were trembling, King Saul was
ready to wage warfare. But he had waited seven long days for
Samuel to come to offer the sacrifice, and his already fearful sol-
diers were scattering. Desperate to stop the attrition he intruded
into the priest's office and offered the sacrifice. He treated the sacrifice as a mere formality, and in so doing failed to reverence God
and entered into disobedience. He failed to see that obedience to
God was the first condition to his being king.

Waiting on God will test your patience, and the flesh will
scream out for action. If you want to hear God's voice when you
don't know what to do you must stand still and wait for His timing.

Farmers have formulas for planting,
    BUT NOT FOR REAPING.
Planting is in our hands,
    and reaping is *in God's hands.*

I planted, Apollos watered, but God [all the while]
    was making it grow and [He] gave the increase.
So neither he who plants is anything
    nor he who waters, but [only] God
Who makes it grow and become greater.

1 CORINTHIANS 3:6, 7

GOD HAS GIVEN you the great honor and responsibility of planting the seed of the Word of God in the lives of those you contact. But it is a great mistake to think you are also responsible to reap the harvest. To compare Paul as the planter and Apollos as the waterer of the Word is like comparing two candles and then watching the sun rise in the morning. It is because there is a Christ that there is a church. You must do your part but if there is any light or joy or love it is because of God, not you. You may plow the field and drop in the seed but you did not make the field or the seed. It is God's field and God's seed, His truth, His wisdom and His will. You can count on success because God has the power to reap what you have faithfully sown.

If you will *trust God*
AS YOUR SOURCE,
He will trust you with *His Resource.*

But you shall [earnestly] remember the Lord
your God, for it is He Who gives you power
to get wealth, that He may establish
His covenant which He swore to your fathers,
as it is this day.

DEUTERONOMY 8:18

GOD HIMSELF IS the great source of power and wisdom and wealth. He has the power to "command the blessing upon you in your storehouse and in all that you undertake. And he will bless you in the land which the Lord your God gives you" (Deuteronomy 28:8). Believers are to be a supernatural people who live under the fullness of God's blessing through faith and obedience to the Word of God. Why do so many struggle to believe God delights in giving His children the power to gain wealth?

The blessing of God includes everything connected with your life—your body, your soul, your family, your service to God, your work and your wealth. By faith you need to put your complete trust in God for all He has for your life including your wealth. Faith rises above whatever circumstance you find yourself in. It triumphs over every challenge. If you trust Him as your only source and give Him all the glory, He will trust you with His resources.

Some say not to be
SO HEAVENLY MINDED
that you're of no earthly good.
Yet many are *so earthly minded*
they are of *no heavenly good.*

And after He had dismissed the multitudes,
He went up into the hills by Himself to pray.
When it was evening, He was still there alone.

MATTHEW 14:23

IF JESUS CHRIST must be alone in prayer, do you really think you can do without it? On the solitary mountain, He came before His Father in heaven to commune face-to-face. Jesus taught by example that your spiritual life must be renewed day by day. You must have your times of being alone with your Father if you would have your heart filled with peace and your mind opened to the daily revelation that God gives to those who love Him.

If you seldom give God time enough to reveal Himself to you, you seldom experience the power of the true knowledge of God. It is good to be silent before God in prayer that He may reveal Himself. By His hidden but mighty power God will manifest His presence to you. To know God in the personal experience of His presence and love is life indeed. You must be closed in with God.

God wants to make His interests
YOUR INTERESTS,
not your interests His interests,
unless your interests
have become *His interests.*

Pray, therefore, like this: Our Father
Who is in heaven, hallowed (kept holy)
be Your name. Your kingdom come,
Your will be done on earth as it is in heaven.

MATTHEW 6:9, 10

CHRISTIANS FROM all backgrounds and persuasions have always found common ground in the Lord's Prayer. Notice that true prayer does not begin with your pouring out a list of your desires and wants to God as if He is a waiter in a restaurant, but with "Our Father." Prayer must begin with the spirit of a child who cries, "Abba, Father" (see Romans 8:15). It begins with knowing God as Father, reverencing His name and coming before Him with love and godly fear.

Fundamental to our Lord's Prayer is making His interests your interests and not vice versa. He is your Father and you are a child of the King, and His will for you is best even if it leads through difficulties and pain. How foolish to try to bend His arm to get Him to give you what He knows may be harmful to you. In heaven the angels are always doing His will in obedience to His commands. May you be quick to do the same.

Your mouth is the
DOORWAY
to the expression of *your soul.*

For the Word that God speaks is alive and full
of power [making it active, operative, energizing,
and effective]; it is sharper than any two-edged sword,
penetrating to the dividing line of the breath
of life (soul) and [the immortal] spirit, and of joints
and marrow [of the deepest parts of our nature],
exposing and sifting and analyzing and judging
the very thoughts and purposes of the heart.

HEBREWS 4:12

THE WORD PICTURE drawn by the writer of Hebrews is that of a sacrificial victim being prepared to face the sharp edge of the high priest's knife. In this case it represents the action of the Word of God to pierce so deeply into your life that it exposes what is merely of the soul in your life—your own opinions and actions—and what is born of the Spirit.

Listen to your words, for your words reflect the thoughts of your soul. Do not fear to bring them under the scrutiny of the Word of God. Your great High Priest is Jesus. Whose only intent is to supply you with His grace and shape your life for His glory. Let His Word expose and sift and analyze and judge your thoughts and the purposes of your heart.

An attitude is a way of life
formed by *negative or positive*
DECISIONS MADE
in the midst of circumstances
we are *experiencing or have experienced.*

Eat not the bread of him who has a hard,
grudging, and envious eye, neither desire his dainty
foods; for as he thinks in his heart, so is he.
As one who reckons, he says to you, eat and drink,
yet his heart is not with you [but is grudging the cost].

PROVERBS 23:6, 7

SOLOMON SPOKE OF a host who from all outward appearances seems to be generous and friendly, but who in his heart is grudging the cost and hard and envious. Beware of the person who does not give freely, for as that man thinks in his heart, so is he. What a man thinks determines what he feels and how he behaves, and his envious, begrudging attitude about life has been shaped by past decisions.

What you think in your heart determines your behavior. If your thinking and attitudes are based upon faith and truth you are going to experience success. Jesus said, "According to your faith and trust and reliance [on the power invested in Me] be it done to you" (Matthew 9:29). Failure or victory is conceived in your thinking firsts then birthed in your life.

Are you in competition
WITH OTHER PEOPLE
or in compassion with other people?

As Jesus landed, He saw a great crowd waiting,
and He was moved with compassion for them,
because they were like sheep without a shepherd;
and He began to teach them many things.

MARK 6:34

WHAT IS IT you love most about Jesus Christ? Probably the same characteristic that drew the massive crowds to follow Him into the wilderness—His compassion. It was the keynote of His life. Wherever He went, He was moved with sympathy and pity to heal, deliver, feed, clothe, and restore those in need to wholeness. Compassion was behind every miracle He did. This is His power over the world and His power over you. You love Him because He has brought His compassion to your life.

If Jesus lives inside you, if He rules your personality, He will make compassion, not competition, the keynote of your life. "For the love of Christ controls and urges and impels us" (2 Corinthians 5:14)—this is a heart attitude that fills you with blessing. Attitude is the determining factor between being blessed and being miserable.

May the Holy Spirit fill you with His compassion to bring His life and touch to those in need around you.

A *negative attitude* that comes from
TRUSTING SELF
will look at *a situation*
that needs an answer
and call it *a problem.*

And they said to me, The remnant there in the province
who escaped exile are in great trouble and reproach;
the wall of Jerusalem is broken down, and its [fortified]
gates are destroyed by fire. When I heard this,
I sat down and wept and mourned for days and fasted
and prayed [constantly] before the God of heaven.

NEHEMIAH 1:3, 4

NEHEMIAH WAS AN exiled Jew who had become a trusted servant of the Persian King Artaxerxes. Hearing of the troubles of those who were in Israel and that the walls of Jerusalem were broken down, Nehemiah was driven to prayer and fasting and profound grief. He could have pointed to several scriptures and said the problems in Jerusalem were because of God's judgment for sin, and he would have been right. But he totally identified himself with his people and was moved with passion to come before God for an answer to this dreadful situation. And it was out of that passion for Zion and God's honor that God raised up Nehemiah to see the walls restored.

If you bring a positive attitude that comes from trusting God you will look at what others call a problem and see a situation for which there is an answer.

Good *thoughts* must be chosen;
THEY WON'T JUST FALL
into your mind.

For the rest, brethren, whatever is true, whatever
is worthy of reverence and is honorable and seemly,
whatever is just, whatever is pure, whatever is lovely
and lovable, whatever is kind and winsome
and gracious, if there is any virtue and excellence, if there
is anything worthy of praise, think on and weigh
and take account of these things [fix your minds on them].

PHILIPPIANS 4:8

THE APOSTLE PAUL was well aware of the power of your thought life. Your thoughts are the foundation upon which your actions and character are built. Negative thoughts will cause you to get upset and confused and will lead you into doubt and unbelief. Negative thoughts will keep you from experiencing the abundant life Jesus has for you. A negative thought is a dose of death. Thinking good thoughts involves a choice; they don't just fall into your head. And it is not merely thinking the right thoughts but continuously appropriating them into your life. If you are careful with your thought life, it will mold your character positively and guard your heart from deception.

Doing the right thing
with a WRONG ATTITUDE
equals *bad results.*

Woe to you, scribes and Pharisees, pretenders
(hypocrites)! For you give a tenth of your mint
and dill and cummin, and have neglected
and omitted the weightier (more important)
matters of the Law—right and justice and mercy
and fidelity. These you ought [particularly]
to have done, without neglecting the others.

MATTHEW 23:23

TITHING WAS BUT one of a long list of "right things" the Pharisees did that Jesus pointed out as coming out of hearts of hypocrisy and thus yielding bad results. The fact that they were detailed in their tithing down to the herbs in their gardens was not a reflection of their love for God. They did it to impress others around them. This practice only fueled their pride, hypocrisy, and self-righteousness. Jesus did not say they should stop tithing but He let them know they were missing the point completely. What value was the tithing of herbs compared to "right and justice and mercy and fidelity"?

Jesus' word to you is that to perform certain acts that look righteous while cheating your neighbor or refusing mercy to others is to deceive yourself. It is to walk with the same spiritual blindness of the scribes and Pharisees. Beware of the blindness that accompanies doing "right things" with a wrong heart.

When you complain,
YOU OPEN THE DOOR
for the devil and *close the door*
to the answer.

And the Lord said to Moses and Aaron,
How long will this evil congregation murmur against Me?
I have heard the complaints
the Israelites murmur against Me.

NUMBERS 14:26, 27

IF YOU READ through Numbers 14 you will understand the severity of the Israelites' complaint that had pushed God's forbearance to the breaking point. Not only were they purposing to pick a new leader who would take them back to slavery in Egypt, they were even considering stoning Joshua and Caleb! Their complaint was born from unbelief and rebellion which open the door for the devil and close the door to God's answer of faith.

The fear instilled by the report on the Promised Land always takes away the full picture and darkens the soul. The spirit of fear colors everything it touches with death and helplessness. Dread is only destroyed by obeying God without delay. The key is to do what Joshua and Caleb did: Trust in the promises of God and allow God to work the miracles required for victory.

Give in secret. If you are to
RECEIVE A REWARD,
you cannot blow your own trumpet.
Whoever blows his trumpet
blows his reward.

Thus, whenever you give to the poor, do not blow
a trumpet before you, as the hypocrites in the
synagogues and in the streets like to do, that they may
be recognized and honored and praised by men.
Truly I tell you, they have their reward in full already.

MATTHEW 6:2

THE PHARISEES divided their practice of religion into giving to the poor, prayer, and fasting. In all these areas they were characterized by Jesus as performing their religious duties for the sake of showing off. The Greek word for "hypocrite" means "stage actor," which is essentially what they were. Their giving was not from a sense of obedience to God, let alone compassion, but that their good works might be trumpeted for all to see and honor.

If that is your motive for giving, Jesus says, "You have your reward already." You may impress others but you will have no reward from God. If your motive in giving is to offer it as a sacrifice to Christ, Jesus said that though you give in secret, "Your Father Who sees in secret will reward you openly" (Matthew 6:4). Do what is right and God will do the rest.

Fear of giving
HINDERS YOUR FREEDOM
of living.

There are those who [generously] scatter abroad,
and yet increase more; there are those who withhold
more than is fitting or what is justly due,
but it results only in want. The liberal person
shall be enriched, and he who waters
shall himself be watered.

PROVERBS 11:24, 25

WHILE MUCH ATTENTION is given to personal finances today, many people are so consumed by living for themselves that they have little to give—little in comparison with what it should be. Credit-card debt and extending themselves beyond their limits take away not only the money they need for themselves but what they should be giving to God. Selfishness and fear lead to a sort of financial suicide.

By God's own declaration, if you give from the right motives you will be repaid by the Lord. He who opens his hand in loving obedience to God will meet God coming to him with blessings unimagined. "Give, and [gifts] will be given to you; good measure, pressed down, shaken together, and running over, will they pour into [the pouch formed by] the bosom [of your robe and used as a bag]" (Luke 6:38). Don't be so busy trying to keep what God has given you that you miss what God is trying to give you.

If you live in the prosperity of
TOMORROW
today, you may live
in poverty *tomorrow.*

He who cultivates his land will have plenty of bread,
but he who follows worthless people and pursuits will
have poverty enough. A faithful man shall abound
with blessings, but he who makes haste to be rich
[at any cost] shall not go unpunished.

PROVERBS 28:19, 20

YOU AND I live in a time when credit cards and home-equity loans and second mortgages make living beyond our means all too easy. It may even be that you have reason to think your business is about to turn the corner or that the promotion is on the way. Living on that speculative prosperity today is a dangerous game to play. And living on the empty promises of fast, easy money is a certain ticket to poverty.

God's principle for prosperity is that you work hard in obedience to His will for your life. Land, for instance, will yield only in proportion to the labor of the farmer. The more faithful the labor, the greater the blessing—God's promise is abundance. But if you are caught up in finding an easy way to get what you desire you'll be distracted from being faithful to God's will for your life today. Return to faithfulness now, before judgment comes.

The limits of gifts are
ESTABLISHED BY GOD.
The limits of giving
are established *by man.*

*Let each one [give] as he has made up his own mind
and purposed in his heart, not reluctantly or
sorrowfully or under compulsion, for God loves (He
takes pleasure in, prizes above other things,
and is unwilling to abandon or to do without) a cheerful
(joyous, "prompt to do it") giver [whose
heart is in his giving].*

2 CORINTHIANS 9:7

GIVING TO GOD financially begins with the foundational principle that "you were bought with a price [purchased with a preciousness and paid for, made His own]"—that price being the precious blood of Jesus (1 Corinthians 6:20). All you have and ever will have belongs to Him and you are merely a steward of what He has given you in this life.

Paul has compared your giving to the sowing of seed. Believers should give freely and generously as a farmer who knows that every seed planted will yield a harvest. The amount given should not be from a legalistic spirit but from a heart of joy as children of God, from love and gratitude to Jesus Christ. Giving is meant to be a joyful part of your relationship with the Father in heaven. If your offering doesn't touch you, it won't touch God.

Deception is a result of EXALTING YOUR OPINION *above* the Word of God.

Then Peter took Him aside to speak to Him privately and began to reprove and charge Him sharply, saying, God forbid, Lord! This must never happen to You! But Jesus turned away from Peter and said to him, Get behind Me, Satan!

MATTHEW 16:22, 23

UPON HEARING Jesus explain that He must go to Jerusalem to suffer and die and be raised on the third day, Peter immediately rose up to take Jesus aside to demand that these events must not happen. Peter obviously believed he knew better than the Word of God what should happen. In that moment he crossed over into a dangerous deception that Jesus moved quickly to quench.

In a remarkable motion Jesus turned away from Peter and declared that the voice that had just spoken was the voice of Satan. Using almost the same words He used with the devil in the wilderness temptation (Matthew 4:10), Jesus revealed that the temptation to avoid the cross was all too real and that hearing such things from Peter's loving, though misguided lips made it even more difficult. Ignorance of one's own heart is the worst kind of ignorance and easily leads to deception. The only safe place is to believe the Word of God and stand behind its truths.

Confrontation is a two-way street;
no one has the RIGHT-OF-WAY
unless they are *willing to yield.*

Open rebuke is better than love that is hidden.
    Faithful are the wounds of a friend, but the kisses
of an enemy are lavish and deceitful.

NO ONE WANTS to wound their friend but there comes a time when confronting something in your friend's life or in an associate's life is the only appropriate expression of your love for them. It is for their good that it must be confronted and it is born from a heart that is broken and open to the other person. Such a love refuses all falsehood and deceitful words and actions. The confrontation is spoken with clarity and passion, and the confronter must be willing to be confronted in return.

If you find yourself in this difficult position it is always best to confront in private (Matthew 18:15). But there are times when others are being hurt and an open confrontation may be necessary (Galatians 2:11). The power of your confrontation is the spirit and truth from which you delivered it.

The devil likes
to set you up
TO BE UPSET.

And the servant of the Lord must not be quarrelsome
(fighting and contending). Instead, he must be kindly
to everyone and mild-tempered [preserving the bond
of peace]; he must be a skilled and suitable teacher,
patient and forbearing and willing to suffer wrong.
He must correct his opponents with courtesy
and gentleness, in the hope that God may grant that
they will repent and come to know the Truth
[that they will perceive and recognize and become
accurately acquainted with and acknowledge it].

2 TIMOTHY 2:24, 25

YOU MAY FOOL others regarding your weaknesses, but you will not fool the devil. He watches long and hard and knows precisely where the weaknesses are in your armor. Samson may have thought it was a game he was playing with Delilah but it was only a matter of time before his point of vulnerability was exposed. And once exposed Satan will exploit that weakness whenever he needs to. He will continually work to set you up to be upset and lose the effectiveness of your Christian testimony. If he can provoke you to being contentious and angry with others, if he can work it so that you are harsh or impolite, he knows the light of truth will be dimmed so that others will not come to repentance. Do not underestimate your adversary—he knows what he's doing.

Negative situations are
NOT PERMANENT,
so why should you *allow your mind*
to be *ruled by them?*

For I am persuaded beyond doubt (am sure)
that neither death nor life, nor angels
nor principalities, nor things impending and threatening
nor things to come, nor powers, nor height nor depth,
nor anything else in all creation will be able
to separate us from the love of God
which is in Christ Jesus our Lord.

ROMANS 8:38, 39

AS YOU READ these powerful words from Romans 8 keep in mind they came from the apostle Paul. Consider his life experience as expressed through the Book of Acts, and you realize that this was a man who was tested by adversity and negative situations on a grand scale. He suffered at every level a person can suffer both from those outside the church as well as from some inside the church. Having faced the worst Paul refused to allow these situations to rule his life because he knew that however much they might affect his life they could not separate him from the love of God.

Your overcoming strength in life is that God is for you and that your risen Lord and Savior has opened the door to His love and care that cannot be shut by anyone or anything else.

Are you dependent on God
or INDEPENDENT OF GOD?
Whichever you choose
will determine *your mood.*

Why are you cast down, O my inner self?
And why should you moan over me and be
disquieted within me? Hope in God and wait
expectantly for Him, for I shall yet praise Him,
Who is the help of my [sad] countenance, and my God.

PSALM 43:5

DAVID TALKED TO God about how he was feeling and so
should you. His prayer life dealt with the real issues he was facing
and so should yours. How you approach God with every aspect of
your life will profoundly impact your mood. Even your prayer life
can simply be rote rather than a reflection of a true dependence
upon God. They are as different as darkness and light.

The fact that you put your faith in God does not necessarily
change the things around you that are affecting your life, but it
changes you. It reaches deeply into your joy and peace. It allows
you to move forward with the assurance that you know Him and
that He knows you. It allows you to focus on the goodness of God
and not just on what is troubling your thoughts and weighing you
down. Hope in God and open your heart to praise Him today!

SUBMIT

If you will *submit yourself* to God,
        you will loose the Holy Ghost
IN YOUR BEHALF.

Therefore humble yourselves [demote, lower yourselves
        in your own estimation] under the mighty hand
of God, that in due time He may exalt you,
    casting the whole of your care [all your anxieties,
        all your worries, all your concerns, once and for all]
            on Him, for He cares for you affectionately
        and cares about you watchfully.

1 PETER 5:6, 7

THERE ARE FEW people who are more miserable than those who have enough Christianity to save them but not enough to transform them. Those who have not received the fullness of the Holy Spirit are missing the joy of the Lord and His strength for daily living. It is like living on crumbs in poverty when the loaf of bread is on the table in front of them.

Paul once asked the Ephesian disciples of John, "Did you receive the Holy Spirit when you believed [on Jesus as the Christ]?" (Acts 19:2). Humble yourself before the Lord and ask yourself that question. Are you filled with the power of the Holy Spirit? Has He transformed your life by grace and is He ruling in your heart? If He is not, open your heart to Him and receive the Holy Spirit now. He only awaits your prayer.

Why do you get frustrated?
BECAUSE YOU ARE TRYING
to be the *Holy Spirit.*

But it is from Him that you have your life
in Christ Jesus, Whom God made our Wisdom
from God…our Righteousness…and our
Consecration…and our Redemption.

1 CORINTHIANS 1:30

THE HOLY SPIRIT is the source of all your spiritual life—all of it. It follows, then, that you'll be frustrated if you attempt in any way to manufacture your spiritual life. This is especially true when it comes to overcoming sin. Believers are said to have "cleansed their hearts by faith" (Acts 15:9)—you are saved from sin through grace by means of faith not by works. The Holy Spirit comes to dwell within you by faith. It is faith that works by love. It is by faith that you overcome the world, the flesh, and the devil. It is by faith that you fight the good fight and quench the fiery darts of the enemy. Only the power of the Holy Spirit within you can save you from sin, and faith is the condition of His working. By faith receive His cleansing influence and allow Him to shed His love abroad in your heart that will sustain you in victory over sin.

DAVE MEYER

Dave Meyer is the husband of Joyce Meyer and business administrator of Joyce Meyer Ministries. He is a veteran of the United States Army and held a career in engineering prior to joining Joyce in ministry. Dave actively pursues his belief that people of faith have a right and responsibility to be involved in the world around them. He is keenly aware of the profound influence of Christianity upon America's early founding fathers and upon the framers of the United States Constitution. Dave's deep conviction of the unique blessing of liberty, self-government, and union bequeathed to Americans, and his passion to hand this understanding down to the next generation, lead him in his involvement in community, social, and political arenas.

TO CONTACT DAVE MEYER WRITE:

JOYCE MEYER MINISTRIES
P.O. Box 655
Fenton, MO 63026
or call: (636) 349-0303

Internet Address: www.joycemeyer.org

In Canada, write:
JOYCE MEYER MINISTRIES CANADA, INC.
Lambeth Box 1300
London, ON N6P 1T5
or call: (636) 349-0303

In Australia, write:
JOYCE MEYER MINISTRIES—AUSTRALIA
Locked Bag 77
Mansfield Delivery Centre
Queensland 4122
or call: (07) 3349 1200

In England, write:
JOYCE MEYER MINISTRIES
P.O. Box 1549
Windsor
SL4 1GT
or call: (0) 1753-831102